THE WAR ON FUN

EZRA LEVANT

Western Standard
Calgary, Alberta

THE WAR ON FUN

Copyright © 2005, Ezra Levant

First printing 2005

National Library of Canada Cataloguing in Publication

Levant, Ezra, 1972-
War on fun/Ezra Levant.

Includes bibliographical references and index.
ISBN 0-9739541-0-8

1. Liberty. 2. Social control--Canada.
3. Social control—United States. I. Title.

JC585.L374 2005   323.44   C2005-906542-7

For more information or to order copies, contact:
WESTERN STANDARD
Att: The War on Fun
1550 Fifth Street SW, Suite 205
Calgary, Alberta, Canada
T2R 1K3
TOLL FREE 1-866-520-5222
Website: www.westernstandard.ca/waronfun

Printed in Canada by Western Standard

TABLE OF CONTENTS

TABLE OF CONTENTS

Prologue: Father Cigar

Rev. Matthew Weiler was fresh out of divinity school when he accepted a post at Manhattan's Saint Mary the Virgin church. The young priest from small-town Florida arrived in New York City to take up his responsibilities on September 1st, 2001. Ten days later, terrorists flew two hijacked airliners into the World Trade Center.

Right across the street from Ground Zero is St. Paul's Chapel, a sister church to Rev. Weiler's own, and the oldest continuously used building in New York. Miraculously – that's what Rev. Weiler would say – not a single pane of glass in St. Paul's was broken. Not a single tile on the roof was blown off.

St. Paul's immediately became a base camp for disaster relief, especially for clergymen like Rev. Weiler. "As soon as everyone could catch their breath," he says, "it became the center."[1]

St. Paul's was within the secure perimeter around Ground Zero set up by the FBI, "but we didn't have to apply for permits, since it was one of our churches, right there." If Rev. Weiler had been wondering why providence had sent him to New York that September, he had found his answer.

"It was organized chaos," he says of the first days after the attacks. "Firemen from all over the country just started driving to New York. Hope was pretty high that we would find people alive." Emergency workers came to try to rescue other emergency workers; and when too many days had passed to keep hoping to find anyone alive, they still kept searching, as Rev. Weiler puts it, "to help dig the image of God out of the pit." He showed up too, "hoping that I could be of service in some way."

Everyone was doing what they could to help. Brusque New York became a city of volunteers. Restaurants from all

5

over the city – all over the country, in fact – began sending food to the St. Paul's relief site, sometimes addressed just to "New York, New York – World Trade Center." Other gifts were less useful; stuffed toys arrived by the dozen. A rumour circulated that police dogs sniffing for survivors had run out of dog food, so hundreds of Americans started sending that, too. Whatever people thought might ease the pain, ease the burden, they did, or tried to do.

"I knew this was going to be hard," says Rev. Weiler, thinking back on his first visit to Ground Zero, just three days after the attacks. "I had been a chaplain at a hospital. I had people die on me." Of course, no one had the experience to prepare them for 9/11. Still, he says, "I figured I could be of some help."

I MET THESE FIREMEN

What is Hell like? That is a question to ask a priest. And if St. Paul's Church had become an island of ministering angels, across the street from it – a street called Church Street, no less – was a burning crater in which thousands of innocents had perished.

"There was a constant fire burning in that pit," says Rev. Weiler. "It had a kind of apocalyptic quality. The air was thick with the smoke and the stench. Like everyone else, I was horrified by the atmosphere, and the conditions in which these people were tirelessly laboring." St. Paul's quickly became a place where those laborers could come for a brief rest, to get food and water, to sit for a minute, and maybe to pray with a young priest.

"The people on the inside of the perimeter weren't allowed to leave. You couldn't come and go. These people were essentially on 24 hours a day duty," says Rev. Weiler. Many just didn't go home. And there weren't a lot of places to have a break. Certainly no convenience stores or cafes – those that weren't destroyed were sealed off by authorities.

One of the first days after 9/11, Rev. Weiler ventured into the pit itself. "I put on some black trousers, and my clerical collar, and I headed down there. We got some wheelbarrows, loaded them up with bottles of ice water and other drinks, and went into the pits." A month earlier, the thought that he would be wearing a hard hat and rubber boots, handing out drinks in a war zone in New York would have been unthinkable.

"We headed out, that day, encouraging people, giving them drinks – Gatorade, Frappucinos, drinks that people had donated. Whatever it was, we loaded it up," he says. The air was thick with the foulest soot and dust and smoke; most relief workers wore face masks. Rev. Weiler tried something different. "I chomped on a cigar," he says. "It filtered out the asbestos in the air just as good as any 5 cent mask, and frankly it cut down on the smell in the air, which was pretty disgusting." He took along a couple of extra cigars in his pocket, too.

As they started making the rounds, Rev. Weiler spotted a hook and ladder firetruck from Dade County, Florida. "And since I didn't really know who to walk over to, I headed over to the firemen, and asked, 'Would you like a drink?'"

"I told them I was from Florida, too," says Rev. Weiler. It was surely just as comforting for him to meet people from back home as it was for the firemen – a feeling of familiarity, of community. "I wasn't in New York much longer than these guys," he says. "I told them I had just moved to New York two weeks earlier. They said, 'Hey, good timing, Father!'" But of course, for a priest, it was good timing.

One of the Florida volunteers wasn't listening much – he was just staring at the priest's cigar. He took a bottle of ice water, says Rev. Weiler, "but he said 'I could really use a smoke right now. I'm stuck here. We could really use these cigars. Everyone's sending us stuff that we don't really need.'" After a week in the burning pits, Frappucinos just weren't enough.

Rev. Weiler only had the one extra in his pocket; he handed it over. "And then it hit me: He's probably not the only one."

"It came as a surprise to me that they couldn't really leave, and of course, everything was shut down. All the businesses – they were all closed. These guys were working in the midst of this disgusting and apocalyptic horror and I thought they ought to have what they really need."

Some prayers can only be answered by God's angels; others can be answered by men of action and ingenuity. Or maybe that is the same thing. "I'll do what I can," Rev. Weiler told the sooty firemen. "So after I left, I visited some cigar stores. The place I always go to get my cigars is J.R. Tobacco on 46th and 5th Avenue. So I went down there, because I come in once a week. They know me – after all, how many priests are regular cigar buyers?" he jokes.

"I talked to the manager. Everyone in New York was chipping in. You couldn't believe how friendly people were. People would have given their right arm to help in any way." And Rev. Weiler knew what at least one fireman from Florida wanted: a good cigar.

"I was down *there*," Rev. Weiler told the tobacconist, though his grimy yellow rubber boots already had communicated the same thing. "I met these firemen…" But before he could even finish his sentence, the whole store staff knew what they had to do. "What do you need?" they interrupted. Rev. Weiler told the story of his day, of the firemen's simple request. "Absolutely," said the manager. "Come back tomorrow and I'll see what I can do."

Rev. Weiler mentioned his errand for the Dade County firemen to one of his parishioners, who set about a duplicate cigar hunt herself, at all of her favourite haunts. Later that night, Rev. Weiler stopped into a bar next to his own church in mid-town Manhattan, to watch the President's address on television. Everyone saw his yellow rubber boots, and the grime, and the bartender asked how the work was going. "Do they have things that they need?" she asked.

"I happen to be rounding up cigars," he said, a little tentatively. "Great!" came the reply from the half the room. "We'd like to contribute something." For a shocked, grieving city, it was a small but concrete way to support the angels who had come from around the country to help. Pretty soon, Rev. Weiler had a huge stack of cigar boxes from all over Manhattan.

"I got stacks of these things. We would go down there, 12 hour shifts, one member of the clergy, about a dozen parishioners, we'd serve meals. I'd grab a couple of boxes of cigars from this stack, and we'd take it down.

"THERE IS A GOD!"

"I came back down two days after I had first spoken to the Dade County firemen," he recalls. "I was maybe a hundred yards away and they saw me coming, these same firemen. And I held up a cigar box in my hand, and I happened to be chomping on one at the time, too," laughs the priest.

"And that's when one fireman yelled out 'There is a God!' as a kind of ecstatic utterance that I'd finally come through on my promise and I held up the boxes," says Rev. Weiler.

"Yes, and I work for him!" shouted back the priest above the din. They all erupted in gales of laughter, perhaps for the first time since September 10th. They felt human again. They felt a trace of normalcy again. Of comfort. The young priest's small errand had brought some small joy. But in those early days, New Yorkers took their joy in whatever size they could find it.

Rev. Weiler laughed then, but he cried later. "There they were, covered in ash," he says. "They had just come back from the pit. Every shift they had to change their boots because the hot iron melted them."

"They were a long way from home. With the cigars, they got a little taste of home. Eventually it grew. Word spread. 'Hey, there's a priest handing out cigars.' I kept on handing them out." The bottles of water and the home-made sandwiches were well-appreciated. But the daily cigar break became a treat to be looked forward to with great anticipation.

"They started calling me Father Cigar all over Ground Zero," he says.

"Frankly it was a little thing. I didn't think it was a big deal. Some cigar stores volunteered. Other friends started, too. It spread. People realized that the firemen didn't just need gifts like Chapstick. That's what happened."

It's not easy to always know what the right thing is to do in a crisis. The mind cannot process the horrors of 9/11. But the generosity and hope of the firemen from across America and even Canada who spontaneously came to Ground Zero – well, that is too large to fathom, too. And that generosity and hope was measured one hour at a time; one act of kindness at a time. Father Cigar was part of that.

ENTER THE ANTI'S

But Rev. Weiler wasn't the only one on a holy mission in New York. Word of his cigar runs had made it to the city's anti-tobacco activists. 9/11 or not, they believed Father Cigar had to be stopped.

"There were some nay-sayers," recalls Rev. Weiler. "Some people are extremist about the anti-smoking thing," he says. The anti's didn't try to convince the firemen that they were wrong to want the relief of a smoke. They didn't dare. And they didn't even try to talk the young priest out of his spirited errand. They did what they are best at doing – filing complaints; seeking injunctions; stopping people through orders.

They complained to his superior at the church. They

demanded that Father Cigar be stopped. They petitioned that his cigar runs be cut off.

But he was not deterred. "Most people loved it," remembers Rev. Weiler. "95 per cent of the people thought it was great. And they helped out in their own little way. And apparently it was appreciated by some of those guys. We never failed to hand them out like hotcakes, I'll tell you that!" he laughs.

"Most of them could have used a lot more. And there were a lot of cigarette smokers, too – but I didn't have connections in that regard. These guys were 'jonesing' for nicotine, and it was a very unpleasant environment. I thought it was the least I could do," he says.

Save it, Reverend. The arguments of freedom of choice or personal enjoyment don't work with hard-boiled anti-tobacco lobbyists. To them, these firemen weren't making an adult choice, they were victims – victims of tobacco companies. And they certainly didn't see the young priest as a relief worker. They saw him as an ordained drug-pusher.

But such insults don't faze a man who has walked through the pits of Hell, and looked into the weary eyes of hundreds who volunteered to rescue, and then to bury, the thousands of innocents who died there.

Unhealthy smoke? Don't be ridiculous. "I thought 'I'm breathing in enough asbestos here to give me who knows what disease'. It wasn't a fresh spring day in the country down there, I'll tell you that. The last thing I need is someone giving me the business about health concerns. I just ignored those people," says Rev. Weiler.

"Don't you know those things are bad for you?" asked one anti. "As if enough people haven't died recently," sneered another.

What kind of puritan would stand in a smoky grave – where some of the smoke was human smoke – and chide a weary rescuer for having a cigar on his break?

What kind of crass activist could read the news of thousands of murders, and profane that horrible news, desanctify it, by comparing it to the health risks of the personal choice of smoking?

It irritated Rev. Weiler, but not for long. "I really do think those were in the minority. Those were only the most hardboiled anti-tabagists."

"It wasn't like there were ten-year-old children digging through the rubble, and I was telling them to light up," retorts the Reverend. "These were firemen who were far from home, who asked me to do them a favour, and I said yes, and I tried to keep my word, and they appreciated it. These were people who were in the midst of circumstances more difficult than anyone could imagine, a catastrophic situation, and I like to think that I, in my own small way, helped to give them a moment of respite, a moment of pleasure, in the midst of so much pain."

To Rev. Weiler, this wasn't about public policy. It wasn't about the public at all. It was about small acts of kindness. "One fireman had just come out of the pit. I gave him a cigar; he bit off the end, lit the thing and just said 'aahhhh'. He took off his big heavy fireman's jacket, his face was all grimy. He put up his feet, and he got to rest for an hour before had had to go back and dig for his fellow firemen. He had driven from Miami in the expectation that he might find at least one person alive." That's what this was about.

CHAPTER ONE:
CORRUPTING A CULTURE OF FREEDOM

In the North American culture of freedom, it is politically difficult to promote policies that erode the value of personal choice. Smoking bans, bad-mouthing SUVs and slandering fast food all has an authoritarian, government-knows-best feeling to it that evokes a reflexive skepticism in the public at large. One creative response to this problem by the anti's of the world – activists who are anti-smoking, anti-fast-food, anti-SUV, anti-fun – is to argue that personal lifestyle choices aren't choices at all, but that smokers, junk food eaters and SUV drivers are just gullible consumers who are easily manipulated by scheming corporate executives.

There is a whiff of anti-capitalism in this argument. It is an echo of Noam Chomsky's claim that consumer demand is manufactured by advertising, and that people only want to smoke or eat Big Macs or drive Hummers because of cultural peer pressure. There is a flavor of conspiracy theory to it, too: that a secret group of puppet masters has the ability to sell us things we don't want to buy, a theory that the unsuccessful marketers of the Edsel or New Coke no doubt wished were true.

TURNING ADULTS INTO CHILDREN
But if the anti's are successful – if responsible adults can be made to believe that they are not actually responsible for their own personal decisions, if they are just dupes, consumer robots doing what scheming executives and advertisers tell them to do – then another North American instinct can take over from personal freedom: protecting the innocent. That is, if adults who knowingly choose potentially unhealthy behaviours can be redefined as childlike innocents needing protection from being taken advantage of, then the power of the state to regulate and interfere can be

unleashed with at least grudging public support. We don't let bad people take advantage of poor little orphans and vulnerable widows, do we? We have public guardians to protect the mentally disabled from predators, or even from themselves, right? Don't we owe the same protective smother to poor little overeaters and smokers?

That will be a tempting offer to some people who want to be liberated from the results of their own choices. Some people just can't stand the responsibilities that come with freedom – they'd trade it in for the security of having someone else do the choosing and the thinking.

Yet to most North Americans, this forced infantilization of the consumer public is offensive. And it has a history of backfiring with those who value independence and choice the most – teenagers who are looking to rebel against every authority, especially a do-gooder government telling them that cigarettes and junk food are bad. But the anti's encourage those who don't deeply value their personal autonomy to be morally disengaged from their own lives. For those who always had difficulty in making responsible decisions, having a nanny state is attractive. And if avoiding personal responsibility can also land someone a nice legal settlement, that makes it all the more tempting.

Teaching grown adults to shirk responsibility for their own choices is offensive. But it is also empirically wrong to say that people who engage in pleasant but potentially unhealthy behaviours don't know what they're doing. Take smoking for example, the most conspicuous example. It is just not true that smokers are ignorant about the risks of their habit. Adults who make the choice to smoke are fully aware of the health implications that their choice entails – in fact, far from being child-like naifs, most smokers actually overestimate the health risks of smoking.

SMOKERS OVERESTIMATE THEIR RISKS

Surveys done by public opinion companies throughout the 1980s and 1990s show that smokers greatly overstate the impact of smoking on both life expectancy and the incidence of lung cancer. In a massive 1997 national survey [2] for example, men who smoke said they believed, on average, that their habit would make them die 7.9 years earlier than if they didn't smoke. Women who smoke were even more pessimistic about the effect of their health – they thought they'd lose 12.3 years to their habit.

But the scientific literature on the subject[3] shows that life-long smokers die, on average, 6.6 years sooner than those who don't smoke. There's no doubt that is an unhappy risk – but smokers know about the risk and overestimate it, especially women who nearly double the real risk in their own minds.

This might be difficult for health-obsessed people to understand. How someone could knowingly engage in a risky habit? But everyone has a vice; for most people, there is more to life than longevity. The point is not to deny the risks involved, but to acknowledge that smokers are thoughtful risk-takers, not dupes. Smokers smoke for the same reason that people who "should know better" eat a candy bar for a snack instead of a carrot stick. They're under no impression that it's good for them; but that's an adult choice they want to make. After a generation of health warnings on cigarette packages and other anti-smoking ads, what sentient adult could deny knowledge of such risks?

CREATING A VICTIMHOOD MENTALITY

This creates a challenge for anti-smoking activists in government. How do the anti's attack smoking without attacking smokers themselves and turning smokers against the anti-smoking movement? That is, how do anti's come across as anything more than a nag? And if smokers already know the risks involved and choose to continue smoking nonetheless, what other arguments can be marshalled?

It's a delicate task, and one that many tax dollars have gone into studying. In one $60,000 [4] Canadian study, for example, researchers at the polling firm Environics concluded that "virtually all smokers who participated in these groups were well aware of the health risks associated with smoking. They could readily name a wide variety of smoking-related illnesses such as cancer, emphysema, asthma, heart disease, effects on pregnancy and more... As a rule, smokers felt that they personally knew all they needed to know about the health risks of smoking."[5]

That is how smokers really are – people who know they're taking a health risk, but do it anyways, like people who order cheesecake for dessert at a restaurant instead of the fruit plate. Such people aren't likely to respond well to hectoring – being slightly naughty is part of the fun.

LIGHT AND MILD CIGARETTES

Even when cigarettes are light or mild – the smoking equivalent to a lower-calorie cheesecake – the anti's are outraged. At first that sounds like an odd response: Wouldn't anti-smoking activists be happy that smokers were choosing cigarettes with less of the bad stuff in them? But that's not thinking like a true anti-smoking lobbyist: cigarettes that are marked "light" or "mild" are merely an opportunity to redefine smokers as victims of misleading tobacco companies.

Canada's high priests of anti-smoking activism, known as the Ministerial Advisory Committee (MAC), decided that undermining smokers' sense of personal responsibility and knowledge about their own decisions was the key to turning them into victims – victims in need of MAC's help. According to minutes of their meetings, it is "IMPERATIVE to redirect perceived blame from the consumer (smoker) to the industry – critical in repositioning the consumer and to establish motivation to quit through sentiments of manipulation and anger from shame and guilt."[6] That's why the anti's have, counter-intuitively, started a campaign against the very kind of cigarettes you'd think they'd support – ones with less of the bad stuff in them. The very anti-smoking activists who pressed the industry to bring in mild cigarettes in the first place to make them less unhealthy now blame the industry for implying that mild cigarettes are less unhealthy. Not exactly Spock-like logic.

But this isn't about logic or even health; smokers know that smoking is unhealthy. It's about blame, acknowledge the anti's, because you can't blame the smokers themselves and achieve any of the goals the anti's want to – punitive taxes, lawsuits-of-fortune, or the demonization of businessmen. To do that, say the MAC men – a group paid for and organized by the Canadian ministry of health – citizens have to be made to feel manipulated by tobacco executives.

So the government wants to manipulate citizens into feeling manipulated by cigarette companies. It's tough to keep track of who the good guys are supposed to be here. Blaming political and business opponents has become more important to them than real health issues.

MAC and the anti's have tried to paint light and mild cigarettes as misleading terms, and as just another marketing trick by cigarette companies. But government surveys of smokers show that argument just isn't true. "Almost no one in any of the groups volunteered that they had chosen their cigarette brand specifically on the basis of it being less damaging to their health,"[7] said one government report.

ERODING A HISTORY OF PRIVACY

The United States and Canada have a long tradition of accepting social dissenters – a libertarian approach to tolerance. Many of the early American colonists were religious minorities who felt marginalized in Europe. Canada, too, has a history as a refuge, ranging from British Empire Loyalists after the American Revolution to Canada's more modern pro-immigration policies – including being the universal destination for Vietnam-era draft dodgers. If there is one continent where it is acceptable to zig when authorities tell you to zag, it's ours.

Believe in polygamy? Well, if you don't make a fuss about it, you can live in peace in Utah, or in the British Columbia interior. Smoke pot? It has effectively been decriminalized throughout Canada, and in key U.S. jurisdictions like New York state. One of the reasons why the U.S. and Canada have been such a destination for the world's migrants is because personal tastes are generally not subject to public coercion, as long as they don't affect someone else's freedoms.

To be sure, there is room for moral persuasion. Just because the North American tradition is to have limited government, doesn't mean that political and community leaders can't speak out against what they think is bad behaviour. It is sometimes said that the greatest power of the U.S. president, for example, is the power of the "bully pulpit" – for the president to throw his moral authority behind a cause, without actually passing any laws or spending any money. That is, or should be, the libertarian ideal – a society where much is permissible by law, but where social norms and customs, and personal values, make people choose on their own to live their lives within narrower restrictions than those written down by the government.

The concept of personal moral responsibility has taken a beating in recent years; and the debauchery of so much of the political class has removed them as moral role models. When John F. Kennedy declared after the Second World War that he wanted to join the noble adventure of public life, no-one snickered. That wouldn't be true today.

It's one thing for politicians to have lost their own moral authority; it's entirely another for them to take away their own citizens' moral authority, and seek to replace it with their own. How would Canadians or Americans react if a foreign government tried to impose restrictions on our lifestyles? The question is absurd – it is unthinkable that two of the freest nations in the world would accept such nosiness. But is the idea offensive only if it is foisted on us from abroad, or because of the substance of the idea itself? America was built on personal freedom – before the Stars and Stripes, American patriots flew the Gadsden flag, a coiled rattlesnake with the motto "Don't Tread on Me".

THE CAFFEINE REVOLUTION

One of the grievances set out in the Declaration of Independence was that England had "erected a multitude of New Offices, and sent hither swarms of Officers to harass our people." King George wasn't telling Americans that they couldn't eat fast food—it hadn't been invented yet. But he did levy intolerable taxes on the favourite caffeinated drink of the day: tea.

The Boston Tea Party was more about tax fairness and local government accountability than about soft drink freedom. But tea was symbolic of the personal lifestyle choice of the day.

Canada was not born through a revolution as was the United States, but over the years it has developed a culture of personal choice that even exceeds that of America's in certain realms—the decriminalization of marijuana is one controversial example. How can a Canadian culture that tolerates the use of drugs like that countenance a governmental assault on tobacco, fat and SUV's?

CHAPTER TWO:
LAWYERS OF FORTUNE

Sometimes the war on fun is motivated by do-gooders, especially when it comes to cigarettes and food. It's a given that excess in either of these can be unhealthy. But there are other anti's out there who see the successful approach taken by the food and smoke anti's—and turned it into a business model. Peter Angelos is one of them.

MEET PETER ANGELOS

Angelos is an entrepreneurial lawyer specializing in lawsuits on behalf of massive groups of people—many of whom he has never met, and who don't know that he claims to represent them. He's the master of the class action suit, the archetypical litigator-of-fortune who give lawyers a bad name. He "bid" for the right to sue tobacco companies on behalf of the state of Maryland on a commission basis— no do-goodery here. Angelos' investment paid off: his share of the take was $1-billion, a sum that even Maryland's pliant legislators couldn't pay without blushing. After a long fight against the state legislature, Angelos settled for a more modest $150-million fee.[8]

RE-INVESTING IN NEW LAWSUITS

Angelos had to make do with his nine-figure payout because he faced political pressure—the money was coming from taxpayers, either straight from Maryland's treasury, or in the form of tobacco taxes. But most of his other wins are paid out to him directly from companies and their insurers, at the non-negotiable order of a judge. Angelos made his bones suing doctors and pharmaceutical companies, and his biggest windfall came from smokers. Since then, he has gone high tech: In 2001, Angelos filed a mass tort lawsuit against cell phone companies on behalf of hundreds of thousands of victims.

Of course, those hundreds of thousands of happy, chatty cell phone users didn't know they were victims. They hadn't complained; they didn't even know Angelos was suing on their behalf. That's par for the course in U.S. mass tort lawsuits these days, and it's becoming increasingly common in Canada, too. But Angelos had a new angle this time: even he, himself, didn't know that anything was wrong with cell phones. His lawsuit alleged that there could be some "potential" harm to cell phone users—just that scientists hadn't proved that harm exists yet. But, in the name of the public interest, Angelos stepped forward in Maryland and three other states – asking to be paid on commission, again.

CELL PHONE JUNK SCIENCE

Mere months before Angelos' suit, the *Journal of the American Medical Association* published a study of 469 brain-cancer patients that showed no correlation between cell-phone radiation and cancer. Immediately afterwards, the *New England Journal of Medicine* published a National Institutes of Health study of 789 brain-tumor patients that came to the same conclusion—no cause and effect between tumors and cell phones. And in the biggest study of all, from Denmark, 420,000 cell-phone users were tracked for 13 years. They had cancer rates no greater than the population in general.[9]

TILTING THE PLAYING FIELD

Such lawsuits seem absurd. But, in addition to being one of his states' largest contributors to elected politicians, Angelos has developed a reputation for his close relations with the judges who hear his lawsuits.

Angelos juices his chances for success in court to begin with, by supporting laws that tilt the playing field in favour of lawsuits. For example: laws that allow potential plaintiffs more time to sue will naturally lead to more plaintiffs—and that's good for lawyers like Angelos. Norman Stone, Jr., a state senator who sponsored a law to extend the deadline for anti-asbestos lawsuits, was hired later by Angelos.[10] No word whether or not he collected back pay for his time in office.

And once lawyers file all the lawsuits, they need to have them heard, if the lawyers are ever going to see their payday. The legislature even supported Angelos' demand for five more judges to hear his asbestos cases faster—a request that was granted after Angelos brought Cal Ripken Jr. in for a photo opportunity for legislators.

But tilting the playing field in favour of plaintiffs is only the beginning, and Angelos is nothing if not tenacious. During one asbestos suit, Angelos actually made the judge a job offer right in the middle of the trial. Judge Edward Angeletti accepted a defence motion to recuse himself from the case, and a mistrial was declared.[11] Angeletti didn't take the bribe. But how many other judges didn't publicly disclose Angelos' offers?

Angelos, and lawyers like him, have momentum. Each mega-win provides cash to fuel a business "investment" in a subsequent lawsuit; each win builds up legal precedent for relieving individuals of personal responsibility, or, as in the audacious attempt to flatten cell phone companies, to have the courts accept junk science or junk arguments. A loss – or a mistrial – is a setback. But a single win can pay off enough to cover a lot of losses, even if a sheepish state house claws back a few hundred million in commissions. And more fees and commissions means more donations for sympathetic political candidates – and a reputation that telegraphs to any politician or judge that a golden retirement is available for those willing to change or bend the rules enough.

THE NEW NORMAL

Culturally, wins by lawyers like Angelos lead to an acceptance of previously outrageous legal tactics; once a pro-Angelos legislator goes to work for Angelos, that sort of back-scratching no longer becomes shocking. A few days of media disbelief at an offer to hire a judge gives way to a new reality of lowered expectations in the press and lower standards for government. And finally, of course, are the thousand lawyers and law students who dream of being the next Angelos. And thousands of would-be "victims" willing to hire them on commission, too.

WENDY'S SHAKEDOWN

Would-be victims like Anna Ayala. In the spring of 2005, Ayala stole world-wide headlines by claiming that she found a part of a human finger in a bowl of Wendy's chili—and promptly filed a lawsuit against the fast-food company. The claim had all the hallmarks of a shakedown, and police eventually tracked down the real source of the finger—an associate of Ayala's own husband who had lost it in an industrial accident.[12] It was all a ruse to shake down a big company. It didn't work this time—and an unusually skeptical media dug up evidence that Ayala and her family had filed thirteen similar shakedown lawsuits against large companies in recent years. Wendy's managed to appear in the press how it was: a victim, a target for a con artist and her unscrupulous lawyers. But why does Angelos, who has a longer and more serious record of abusive suits, escape similar ridicule and marginalization?

RECRUITING THE NEXT ANNA AYALA

Litigators like Angelos don't just sit back and wait for the Ayalas of the world to present themselves. They eagerly recruit victims. A consortium of litigators-of-fortune sponsor a website with the benign name of ConsumerAffairs.com.

The website has a strong non-profit flavor to it—like a friendly neighborhood ombudsman, or advice columnist. But according to the site's privacy policy, consumer complaints are forwarded to lawyers standing by for clients. The site isn't completely sneaky; it does list dozen of law firms across the continent who pay for online ads, too.

One happy advertiser is the law firm of Horwitz, Horwitz and Associates of Chicago. Just in case visitors to ConsumerAffairs.com find that site's encouragement to sue too subtle, Horwitz has a pretty clear call to arms— a page on their website that Anna Ayala probably wished she had read: $13 Million For Ladder Accident.[13]

"We recovered what is believed to be the largest settlement ever against a ladder manufacturer," gushes their website. "The present cash value of the settlement was $13 million. We alleged that the ladder was unreasonably dangerous because it used ladder shoes that were constructed of vinyl rather than rubber. We demonstrated that rubber had a higher coefficient of friction than vinyl . . .

"We further alleged that the manufacturer inadequately warned about the 75-degree rule that should be utilized when setting up a ladder. A ladder should be set up at a 4-to-1 ratio."

If only Ms. Ayala had read this site—anyone can find a ladder, and place it against a wall at a ridiculous 45 degree angle—stupidity is obviously not a bar to ladder lawsuits. How much easier would that have been than to have found a human finger? Even if the lawyers took half, that's a helluva payday.

CHAPTER THREE:
CREATING HATE

Successful anti's have discovered that when it comes to the war on fun, there is a place for moral puritanism, but other things work better to wring big paydays out of juries or sympathetic regulations from bureaucrats and politicians. The constant harping of the anti's – the moral self-congratulation of the prohibitionists, the reeking intellectual superiority, the kill-joy of it all—doesn't work all the time. Anti-smoking activists remind smokers—and non-smokers with a laissez-faire attitude about tobacco—of the student everyone knew back in school who reminded the teacher to make sure to give out homework. Those students grow up to be anti-tobacco activists.

Such students weren't very popular in grade school, and they fare even worse as grown-ups. There is very little genuine grassroots or popular support for these prohibitionists—certainly not enough to sustain them financially. That's why they rely so heavily on government subsidies.

Getting financial support from government takes care of the financial problem. But what about the larger, cultural problem faced by anti-tobacco activists—that smokers don't like being hectored, just as grade school students didn't appreciate the brown-nosing?

The anti's are aware of this; they know that ordinary Americans and Canadians treat anti-tobacco messages like they treat unsolicited telemarketers—mildly interesting, but a real pain in the neck.

In short, whatever valid or interesting messages the anti-tobacco lobbyists had was being ignored because the messengers were so unappealing. They were busybodies, minding your business for you, and blaming you for having some fun.

The anti's have found a solution to this: They call it "denormalization."

Denormalization—also known as demonization, or defamation—is a shift in propaganda away from blaming and attacking smokers for smoking, and towards blaming and attacking tobacco companies for selling smokes.

CULTURE OF VICTIMOLOGY

From a propaganda point of view, it's brilliant – blaming a big, evil, impersonal business for causing smoking, rather than individual smokers, might stop some smokers from immediately tuning out the anti-tobacco harping. It's one thing to be nagged about your habits; it's quite another to be told you're the victim of a conspiracy. The first is boring – the second is deliciously interesting, and it appeals to a cultural undercurrent of victimology.

Victimology says that people aren't rational decision-makers; they aren't responsible for the bad things in their lives – other forces are. It's a salve to those with unhappy lives, or to those who just aren't as happy as they think they should be. Instead of asking "What went wrong?" or "What can I do differently?", victimology invites people to ask "Who did this to me?" and "How can I get my revenge?"

Denormalization, as with many new ideas started in California, in the early 1990s. As the Washington Legal Foundation, a public interest law firm described it back then, California's anti-smoking campaign was not an attack "on the dangers of smoking, but on the tobacco industry... these advertisements do not educate about health, but portray tobacco industry officials as merchants of death."[14] Some of these ads – being paid for by tax dollars in the name of public health – employed professional actors to portray tobacco executives as evil.

400 YEARS OF SMOKE AND MIRRORS

Demonization of tobacco—and the people involved in the business—is nothing new. King James I himself invented it four hundred years ago. In 1604, as tobacco imported from the New World became fashionable in the Old, he wrote the dramatically titled "Counterblaste to Tobacco."

It was the era before political correctness, and King James didn't hesitate to demonize smokers by the worst epithets he could find – and back then, that meant comparing English smokers to North American Indians. "what honour or policie can moove us to imitate the barbarous and beastly maners of the wilde, godlesse, and slavish Indians, especially in so vile and stinking a custome?" he asked.[15] Smokers made themselves even more useless, said the King, than a Jew on a religious holiday—a "vile custome brought your selves to this shameful imbecilitie, that you are not able to ride or walke the journey of a Jewes Sabboth."

Calling smokers Indians and Jews didn't work: smoking only grew in popularity. So King James did what so many other politicians would in centuries to come: instead of defeating tobacconists, he became business partners with them. His Counterblaste didn't work, so he put his tax-collectors on the file – increasing tobacco taxes from two pence to six shillings, eight pence per pound of tobacco—a 4,000 per cent tax hike.[16] James said the tax hike was for "the Reformation of the saide Abuses." That's a good example of 17th Century spin-doctoring. It was about the money, not the morals. Smoking was not subject to any legal limitation or fine; but failure to pay James' tobacco tax would "not onelie forfeite the saide Tabacco, but alsoe shall undergoe suche furthere Penalties and corporall Punishmente as the Qualitie of suche soe highe a Coutempte against our Royall and expresse Commaundemente in this mannere published shall deserve." Take that!

King James probably didn't actually want smoking to stop

27

—every autocrat needs a demon to rail against. And there was the tax revenue. Those factors are just as evident in the modern day love/hate relationship between big government and big tobacco.

CHAPTER FOUR:
THE ORIGINAL HEALTH NAZI

Curiously, Adolf Hitler, the murderer of millions, had a fanatical opposition to tobacco – and was himself an abstainer not just from tobacco but also from alcohol and meat. Hitler picked up on King James' theme that tobacco was "the wrath of the Red Man against the White Man."[17] But, as one might expect, the bulk of his anti-smoking demonization was rooted in his anti-Semitism and racism.

"Tobacco Is An Obstacle to Racial Policy," blared one Nazi propaganda ad, with a caricatured sketch of a smoking Gypsy mother. Another popular poster showed a picture of a devilish Jew and a smoking Aryan, with the caption "Tobacco has its victims by the neck; the Jew has his victims by the neck."[18] Other Nazi posters went further: cigarettes weren't just dirty like Jews – cigarettes actually were the tools of Jews, a Jewish plot.

SMOKING AS A POLITICAL STATEMENT

But Hitler's exhortations fell on deaf ears. In 1930, before the Nazis seized power, Germans smoked an average of 490 cigarettes each. By 1940, smoking had more than doubled, to 1,022 cigarettes per German per year, and stayed high throughout the duration of the war.[19] And, like King James, when Hitler discovered he couldn't beat tobacco, he joined it – even going so far as to set up a Nazi brand, called Storm cigarettes, whose proceeds went directly into the coffers of his brown-shirts.[20] So important were cigarette revenues to the Nazis, in fact, that brown-shirts would physically beat retailers and smash the windows of those who sold cigarettes made by Reemtsma, instead of the Nazi brand. When the Nazis purged the brown-shirts, they cut a deal with Reemtsma – they would be allowed to continue manufacturing cigarettes, if they turned over millions of Reichsmarks in protection money to the "Adolf Hitler Fund," used as a personal slush fund for Herman Goering.

The Nazi anti-smoking crusade is instructive in so many ways – because its propaganda was ignored by the public it was supposed to inspire; because, as always, governments were more interested in tobacco tax revenues than any claims about public health; and because it shows that today's campaigns of personal demonization of tobacconists have an ugly lineage.

YOUR BODY BELONGS TO THE FUHRER

Hitler's war on cigarettes also tapped into an age-old theme that tobaccophobes have used since King James' day: the concept that the smoker's body does not belong to him – it belongs to the state.

Hitler believed that all Germans had a "duty to be healthy" – and that the state had a claim on their lungs as much as they did. Nazi slogans included:

"Your body belongs to the nation!"

"Your body belongs to the Fuhrer!"

"You have the duty to be healthy!"

And "Food is not a private matter!"

One Nazi pamphlet in Vienna read, "There are people who have made their bellies their god, who in their greed want both goulash and a big helping of whipped cream before they feel they have had enough. But we industrious German racial comrades know what is at stake! We know that the serious and hardworking German does not live on whipped cream and bananas. This is not the time for gormandizers and hysterics who must have a new dainty every day."[21]

It's not a large step from the state regulating what goes in its citizens' lungs to what goes in their mouths. The same legal principles are involved – the government's power to

30

enforce "public health" versus the individual's right to choose his lifestyle, and his property in his own body. Those who care about the freedom to eat whipped cream but don't lift a finger to protect smoking might find that by the time the state gets around to banning their particular vice, the legal precedent has already been set by the war against tobacco.

In the TV comedy Seinfeld, the popular "soup Nazi" character abuses his customers by treating them gruffly – and telling them what they may or may not eat at his restaurant. Jerry and the gang are entranced by the concept of someone treating their customers like sheep – and the customers loving it.

The soup Nazi was allegedly based on a real restaurant in New York; but smoking Nazis – people abusing anyone who smokes, and telling them what they can or can't do with themselves – really were part of the Nazi party, and Adolf Hitler himself was the chief smoking Nazi.

THE ORIGINS OF JUNK SCIENCE

To Hitler, smoking wasn't just a foul habit – it was national danger, not only to the health of Germany, but to the purity of the Aryan race. He appointed a "Reich Health Fuhrer" and in 1942 endowed the "Institute for the Struggle against the Dangers of Tobacco" at the University of Jena with 100,000 Reichmarks of his own money.

The Institute combined real health science with other less academically rigorous philosophies. As Robert Proctor wrote in his seminal work, *The Nazi War on Cancer*, "Professor Karl Astel, SS member and director of the Jena Institute for Racial Policy and Human Genetics as well as the Institute for the Struggle Against the Dangers of Tobacco, was renowned for striking cigarettes from students' mouths, as part of his campaign against "racial deterioration." Astel's racial hygiene activities in Thuringen

31

included the intense harassment of Jews, homosexuals, and the mentally subnormal, the proposition of a "preventive death sentence" for antisocial elements considered to be potential murderers, and an active role in the establishment of the Nazi euthanasia programmes, in which over 70,000 people deemed to be mentally or physically defective were murdered." Tobacco wasn't just considered the cause of disease; it was considered a political threat, the downfall of society, and a moral evil so heinous that violence – including murder – was not worse.

As one Nazi propaganda magazine put it, "brother national socialist, do you know that your Fuhrer is against smoking and thinks that every German is responsible to the whole people for all his deeds and omissions, and does not have the right to damage his body with drugs?" There was no privacy in Nazi Germany, certainly not the privacy of your own body – especially when racially degenerative substances like tobacco were involved.

Turning Hitler's personal whims into laws may have been well-received by the SS – Hitler was also a vegetarian and an animal rights activist – but ordinary Germans were less than enthusiastic. As Proctor notes, "despite this intense health promotion activity smoking continued to increase. This was recognized at the time, and it was perhaps with some glee that the Berlin correspondent for the *Journal of the American Medical Association...* noted that cigarette consumption increased in 1938 from 609 per head to 676 per head." Perhaps it was all the stress of having SS thugs enforcing the no-smoking rules that caused all of that smoking.

Hitler's smoking bans died with the Nazis, but they were not forgotten. As the "liberal" wave of anti-smoking activism spread across Europe and America, it skipped over Germany. "The association of authoritarian anti-smoking efforts at workplaces, on public transport, and in schools with the Nazi regime remained for a long period in popular memory," notes Proctor. Even if the new anti-smoking police don't resort to violent beatings to make their point, their rationale is the same – your body belongs to the state.

CHAPTER FIVE:
TODAY'S HEALTH NAZIS

A modern example of the Nazi fusion of policemen and health crusaders is the phenomenon of the public health officer. One particularly belligerent officer is Dr. Pete Sarsfield, the medical officer of health for Northwestern Ontario. Sarsfield is a health Nazi, without the violence or racial theories but with all of the same fanatic certainty and on the same utopian crusade to make other people do what he wants. And he wants smoking to end.

A NEW SHERIFF IN TOWN

"The evidence has been in for over a decade that this is a health hazard. This is proven, it's not [an] argument in science anymore," he told Canada's CTV network in an interview, with the unshakable faith of a true believer. Sarsfield had set about passing his own laws, wild west-style, banning smoking, even though the local politicians had chosen not to.[22]

CTV's Seamus O'Regan asked Sarsfield if his total ban wasn't too harsh. But Sarsfield didn't have time for such nuances – to him smoking was black and white, no shades of grey. "So if the evidence has been in for a decade and there isn't any action being taken by governments, I'm not sure who is being harsh," said Sarsfield. "I don't think it's the officials. I think it's governments who are being harsh."

Sarsfield had made himself the government – an unelected, unaccountable, one-man government who summarily dismisses the democratically elected officials in Northwestern Ontario's Kenora-Rainy River district and imposed his own law. He forgot that he worked for them; and that they, in turn, served at the pleasure of the voters. But through a bloodless coup, he turned that around. He effectively fired the "government" – and the voters.

Again, CTV's O'Regan wasn't convinced. "A lot of people are wondering, though, doctor, if you have the jurisdiction to do this when many municipalities don't have anti-smoking bylaws?"

Silly reporter. Don't trouble this crusader with your petty questions about legal authority. Here's how Sarsfield replied: "In the area that I work in there are 19 municipalities, most of whom lack the integrity or the courage – and this is also the case for the provincial government, I might add – to do any action."

So that's all it takes, these days, eh? A lone ranger doctor, who can dissolve the local municipalities – or at least ignore them – simply because, in his mind they "lack integrity." They're all wrong. The municipal government is wrong. The province is wrong. He's right. He'll even tell you so, if you ask him.

O'Regan wasn't buying it. "What about drinking then? Is that next? Will we herald in a new era of prohibition?"

"You can drink, yes. And the health risks, if any, are your problem," said Sarsfield.

O'Regan asked Sarsfield just one more question. It wasn't a question that would normally be put to a medical officer of health. It had to do with public opinion; with how businesses were responding; with democracy. But since Sarsfield was now a one-man government, who else could O'Regan ask? The powerless elected officials?

"Tell me about the reaction there, locally," he asked.

"Restaurants are really embracing this," lied Sarsfield. What did he care? Bankrupt restaurateurs and unemployed waitresses couldn't throw him out in the next municipal elections.

JUDGE, JURY AND EXECUTIONER

But even Sarsfield couldn't finesse bars and bingos. "What they're saying – and I love this part – they're saying 'it's going to hurt our business.'"

Sarsfield loved that part. He loved that he's a one-man wrecking ball tearing through town, and that nobody stopped him. And he got to be on national TV, just like all the chumps who actually had to run for election before wielding the law like a battering ram.

"It may hurt our business so we're not going to take any action," mocked Sarsfield. "I love that. We don't allow that with other parts of the society."

B.C.'S HEALTH NAZIS TAKEN DOWN A PEG

Eventually, such rogues can be stopped. In British Columbia, the provincial Supreme Court struck down a similar ban, this one imposed by the Workers Compensation Board, banning smoking in bars, restaurants, prisons – everywhere. Scott McCloy, of Workers Compensation Board of B.C. – their version of Pete Sarsfield was just as full of hyperbole as his Ontario counterpart. "No worker should be exposed to a known workplace hazard. That's like saying a farm worker should be exposed to pesticides."[23]

Uh, they are exposed to pesticides. And gas jockeys are exposed to gas fumes, and firemen are exposed to smoke. Life is not risk-free, and we don't let self-important crusaders shut down the city because they can't see shades of grey.

Said the judge who struck down the WCB's ban: "where the economic impact is so significant, coupled with severe penalties for non-compliance, public debate is of paramount importance."[24]

Apparently not everyone agrees with the Nero-style health dictatorship of Ontario's Dr. Sarsfield.

Sometimes the politicians do cave in to the public health

officers, though. To get around a smoking ban in Ottawa, bars announced that they were no longer open to the public – they were now private clubs, open only to members and their guests.

"What we have done is we've booked exclusive time," said one bar owner. "Now the city's own bylaw… says that places of public assembly are exempt when being exclusively used."[25] "We have about 40 percent of our organization filled up by nonsmokers. But they're nonsmokers who are tolerant of smokers." The City of Ottawa still sued.

What could be the rationale of such a suit? Everyone at the now-private club had positively signed up for a smoking environment. It was a bar – there were no minors involved. Everyone involved was a consenting adult. It was a private smoking club. And the non-smokers wanted to be there. Cue Dr. Robert Cushman, the Medical Officer of Health for Ottawa: "There will be certain pockets of resistance," he said. Pockets of resistance? Is that how a doctor talks, or a vigilante soldier?[26]

CHAPTER SIX:
WHAT HAPPENED IF NOBODY OBEYED?

With campaigns to bad-mouth tobacco companies in full flight, and crusading health Nazis flushing out "pockets of resistance" how are the anti's doing to stop teenagers from picking up the habit in the first place? Can government programs to denormalize tobacco stop kids from smoking?

THE FULL MONTY

A 15-year, $15-million study by the National Cancer Institute in the United States says no. From 1984 to 1999, the Fred Hutchinson Cancer Research Center in Seattle, Washington studied 40 school districts throughout the state.

Half were the "control group" – they were told to do what they had always done by way of anti-smoking education. The other 20 school districts were given the Full Monty – a rigorous propaganda program that started in Grade 3 and didn't let go of them until Grade 10. Scientists tracked the kids until two years after graduation. This was a major study. And it showed that heavy-handed stop-smoking tactics flopped.

According to Dr. Cathy Backinger of the NCI, the students were subjected to "the social-influences approach" where "kids learn and identify what the social influences for smoking are – such as advertising and peer pressure – giving them skills to resist the social influences and then realizing that it's not the norm that people smoke." In other words, according to Dr. Backinger, the 20 special school districts taught their students that tobacco companies were manipulating them; that they were pawns of advertising companies; that they were slaves to their peer group.

KIDS WILL BE KIDS

The study was huge. Thousands of kids were tracked for 15 full years – even after they graduated. And they weren't just lectured to – those who started smoking, for example, were given smoking cessation services. "The design was impeccable" said Dr. Backinger.

And it didn't work.

Were the results surprising? "It was a surprise inasmuch as this intensive program, using the best that we knew at the time, didn't work... we need to put smoking prevention into a comprehensive approach."[27]

"We need to make sure that we include not only schools but parents and communities."

Hang on. Now parents will have to sit through stop-smoking lectures? Will Dr. Pete Sarsfield now have search warrants to enter our homes, too?

"There is no one silver bullet. Not one thing that is going to work. It has to be everything." Especially if you're going to flush out those pockets of resistance.

UNINTENDED CONSEQUENCES

Before it was struck down by the courts, the British Columbia ban imposed by the unelected Workers Compensation Board had a dramatic effect – though not the one planned. Smokers didn't quit en masse. They just quit going to bars to smoke, and smoked elsewhere instead.

Two weeks after the ban, Tanya Larsen found out that the WCB's promises of booming smoke-free lounges were just propaganda. "It was effective immediately because business is slow," she said. "Because of the smoking ban. I work in a lounge. People aren't coming."[28]

The WCB had set up a toll-free snitch-line so that neighbors could spy on each other, and report each other to the police, secretly. 1,200 complaints were filed in the first week alone.[29] The health Nazis of the 1940s would have been proud.

WHEN PUBLIC HEALTH OFFICERS ATTACK

Sometimes real police officers have to step in and remind public health officers that they aren't on *Law and Order*. Dr. Richard Stanwick, who was Victoria, B.C.'s health officer enforcing its 1999 smoking ban, took it upon himself to do a little undercover work after the ban was implemented. Real *Serpico* stuff.

"We paid a visit to [an] establishment at noontime and did issue a ticket because we did not believe appropriate signage was there," Stanwick said after walking his beat.[30]

Hold on for a second. A doctor is issuing tickets?

And not because someone is smoking, but because the owner of a bar didn't put up the doctor's propaganda?

That wasn't all. As part of Dr. Stanwick's crusade, "our staff returned just as part of an overall media tour... unfortunately, the situation did get a little out of hand last night." They were asked to leave "at the request of the Esquimalt police chief."

So it wasn't just the smoking. Or the signs. It was a crusading doctor – unelected, unaccountable – who took it upon himself to do a victory lap, TV cameras in tow, to the smoking sections of restaurants and bars throughout Victoria who were now under his thumb. Things were looking dangerous, and the real police had to step in lest the good doctor have his stethoscope put somewhere unnatural.

The owner of the bar where Dr. Stanwick's big ego-trip came face to face with reality was blunt. "The MLAs can smoke in their office downtown. Convicted murderers or rapists can smoke in their cells on Wilkinson Road. Yet a war veteran can't smoke in what he considers his residence out at Oak Bay Lodge," said Brian Mayzes.

"I think we're a working man's bar and a working man likes to have a beer after work, sit down and have a smoke if he chooses to." Gee, who could have guessed their reaction to Dr. Stanwick's self-congratulatory victory dance?

CIGARS FOR ME, BUT NO CIGARETTES FOR YOU

There is a cultural issue here, a class issue. On the one hand are the white collar, eat-your-peas busybodies. On the other hand, blue collar smokers. And guess who's telling whom how to live their lives? And to lose their jobs?

"Let's face it," said Christine Page, a waitress in a smoking lounge. "People that don't gamble and don't sit at a bar all day aren't all of a sudden going to start drinking all day and gambling because it's non-smoking."[31] In other words, drive out the smokers, and her lounge isn't exactly going to fill up with Dr. Stanwick and his friends.

Or try a bingo hall. "Look around. All our customers all have a cigarette in their hand, a coffee and a dabber,"[32] notes Sidalia Lynne, a bingo manager in Victoria.

No surprise there. Toronto's smoking ban had the same effect – lots of "collateral damage" to people who can't afford high-powered lobbyists like the anti-tobacco advocates can. Within three weeks of that city's ban, the popular Bloor Street Diner had laid off three employees. "As a waitress, I will be out of work if this law is still in effect one week, two weeks from today," said Eleni Kountourogiannis. "And I am putting an ashtray back out on the table."[33] That's not a Big Bad Tobacco Executive talking. It's a woman trying to earn a few dollars slinging drinks in a bar.

This divide hasn't been lost on Rex Murphy, perhaps the only reporter at the CBC with working class sensibilities: "There's nothing like a good gallop on your moral high horse,"[34] he told CBC viewers one night. "The anti-smoking lobby, for example, has had a great ride recently. They've made moral lepers out of the tobacco companies and have put smoking in public on a par, roughly, with white slavery or watching Jerry Springer . . . puffing for cigars is seen as risqué stylish, up-market and empowering. I think it's a class cleavage: peasants and the lower orders, by and large, smoke cigarettes. They've got to be saved even when they

41

don't want to be. The stylish and the rich, on the other hand, movie star and tycoon — well hell, they're not smoking, they're accessorizing a lifestyle."

Murphy wasn't calling for a crackdown on the rich and famous – he was pointing out how the anti-tobacco activists tended to pick on victims a little less media-savvy than, say, Demi Moore, Sylvester Stallone or Arnold Schwarzenegger, all of whom have appeared on the cover of *Cigar Aficionado* magazine. Murphy's not the only one to point out how the ban punishes the "little people" – *The New York Times'* Bob Herbert wrote a similar article, complaining that countless little cafes and diners in New York are hurting economically because of that city's anti-smoking crusade, but the ritzy Oak Bar at the Plaza Hotel just keeps puffing away in the face of the law.[35] Herbert calls New York's Mayor Michael Bloomberg "an anti-smoking zealot", and complains about the unintended side-effects of the ban – lost business, people loitering noisily in the streets at all hours just to smoke. Herbert went to the Oak Bar and interviewed its patrons and managers – business was up 12 per cent, he said, because smokers sought it out as a haven. "It reminded me of the comment attributed to Leona Helmsley: 'Only the little people pay taxes.'" Herbert wrote. "While the "little people" from the Bronx to Staten Island are dealing with the inconvenience of the ban — not to mention the reduced business for bar owners and substantially reduced tips for bartenders and waiters — the power crowd in the Oak Bar continues to light up in grand style, and the owners are cashing in."

Herbert didn't call for the liberation of the "little people," though, or the salvation of their businesses – he turned from reporter into snitch. "I called the Health Department about the Oak Bar shenanigans, and officials were not amused... Health Department inspectors visited the Oak Bar over the weekend and issued notices of violation." Murphy wanted everybody, rich or poor, to be equal in their freedom. Herbert wanted everybody to be equal in their punishment.

CHAPTER SEVEN:
WHO ARE THE ANTI-SMOKERS?

When a group has a name like "Physicians for a Smoke-Free Canada," it sounds like a pretty respectable bunch. Just ask them: according to their website, they are an "organization of Canadian physicians"[36] – and a "registered charity" to boot. No callow profit motive here!

A CORPORATE SUBSIDIARY

Click on their website's financial reports, and things look as clean as a whistle, too. Not a penny shows up under corporate revenues. It's all altruistic donations.

That's what the public is supposed to see. What they're not supposed to see is the corporate partnership that Physicians for a Smoke-Free Canada has struck with GlaxoSmithKline, the pharmaceutical giant that sells Nicorette gum, Nicoderm patches and even a tasty nicotine lozenge.

SECRET TRUST FUNDS

In September, 1999, Cynthia Callard, the executive director of Physicians for a Smoke-Free Canada, wrote a confidential memo[37] to Elizabeth Lindsay, GlaxoSmithKline's executive in charge of "Market Development – Smoking Cessation" proposing that Glaxo immediately transfer $30,000 to a "trust account" managed by Physicians for a Smoke-Free Canada, in support of their "Y2Quit" anti-cigarette lobbying campaign.

There's nothing wrong with a US$32-billion-a-year multinational drug company investing $30,000 into marketing their stop-smoking drugs. If Glaxo's profit motive happens to coincide with getting people to stop smoking, all the better – that's how Adam Smith told us capitalism would work for the betterment of mankind.

It's not the big drug company whose ethics are in question

here – but rather the allegedly grassroots, allegedly non-profit public health advocates at Physicians for a Smoke-Free Canada who have some answering to do.

Did GlaxoSmithKline simply fork over a five-figure donation – the largest non-governmental donation to the group – out of a sense of charity? Or were there any strings attached? What demands did the drug company place on Physicians for a Smoke-Free Canada? And why was the donation kept a secret from the public, and squirreled away in an Enron-style, off-the-books trust account?

In other words, if there was nothing to hide, why was it hidden?

The answer is obvious: Physicians for a Smoke-Free Canada, and all of the lobby groups like it in Canada and the U.S., thrive only by establishing a media image of uncorruptable public advocates, motivated by nothing but high-minded morality. Profiting by taking hand-outs from large corporations just doesn't square with that holier-than thou image. And if Physicians for a Smoke-Free Canada's adoring public were to find out that Glaxo's products – like Nicorette and Nicoderm — actually contain nicotine themselves, and are in fact merely alternative ways for nicotine addicts to get their cravings, well, there would be a revolt. An anti-tobacco, anti-addiction lobby group taking money – and instructions – from a leading global provider of nicotine? No wonder they set up a secret trust fund.

Some answers to this puzzle are provided in another confidential memo, this one from Cynthia Callard to Health Canada itself.[38] Callard does not refer to Glaxo as a donor. She refers to it as a "partner" – and describes the drug company's role as the senior partner in the deal.

SELLING GUM AND PATCHES

According to the memo, Glaxo's "field staff will distribute material to family physicians" – and that material would be promoting Glaxo's nicotine products with the imprimatur of Physicians for a Smoke-Free Canada. Drug company executives would participate in the design of the program, "provide guidance" and in Callard's words "be the 'arms & legs'" of the program. Physicians for a Smoke-Free Canada would even "underwrite printing/production costs" of Glaxo's brochures.

They must be chuckling over at Glaxo's corporate headquarters in London, England. For a $30,000 secret payment, Physicians for a Smoke-Free Canada subcontracted out a stop-smoking program to one of the world's largest drug companies that just happens to be selling stop-smoking nicotine supplements. Better yet, Glaxo gets the benefit of Physicians for a Smoke-Free Canada's name and non-profit reputation.

Physicians for a Smoke-Free Canada repeatedly boasts that it is transparent and accountable – unlike the tobacco companies that it disparages as secretive. The group is at its most righteous when demanding government grants. In its 2001 request for $195,000 from Canada's federal government, Physicians for a Smoke-Free Canada promised that it "will continue to provide full and transparent accounting of its financial and program activities to its funders and the general public" and that there would be "public full disclosure" of any "revenue source" for projects.

Nicely said. But not done.

Glaxo's deep pockets weren't just a temptation to Physicians for a Smoke-Free Canada. Another self-righteous lobby group, called Action on Smoking & Health (ASH), was seeing the benefits of teaming up with a big business, too.

ASH and Physicians for a Smoke-Free Canada teamed up to go to bat for their big benefactor. One of Glaxo's stop-smoking aids, called Zyban, was available by prescription only – and that meant that, like all other prescription drugs, Glaxo couldn't advertise it publicly in Canada.

In 1999, ASH's executive director, Les Hagen, met with Physicians' Cynthia Callard to talk about lobbying for their sugar-daddy, and pressing Canada's health minister to allow Zyban to be given a special exemption from the ad ban. To see the genius in Glaxo's "market development" strategy, look at it from a politician's point of view: who is a more credible lobbyist for a foreign drug company – a Gucci-wearing drug company consultant, or a couple of Canadian "health advocates"? That was the best $30,000 Glaxo ever spent. Zyban wasn't without its problems – it made headlines in 2002 for a spike in the number of deaths amongst people who were taking the drug. But business is business.[39]

UNCHARACTERISTICALLY TRUSTING

Hagen and Callard were just as thrilled about their new partnership as the drug company was. "I have full confidence that GlaxoWellcome [as Glaxo was called then] will ensure that their promotions are appropriate and beneficial,"[40] Callard wrote. Who knew that Physicians for a Smoke-Free Canada, which regularly demonizes "big tobacco," would be so touchingly trusting of an even bigger pharmaceutical company?

But Callard knew she couldn't let her fulsome embrace of a pharmaceutical company taint Physicians for a Smoke-Free Canada's virginal reputation. After all, she wrote, there is "the risk that we will be perceived as agents of the pharmaceutical sector."

It did not trouble Hagen and Callard that they actually *had* become agents of the pharmaceutical sector, that they had delegated decision-making to Glaxo, asked for and received massive secret donations to hidden trust funds, and rented out their reputation as a non-profit charity to a for-profit nicotine vendor. The reality of their transactions was not their worry.

No. They were just worried that the public would find out

about it.

FEAR OF PUBLIC SCRUTINY

The vitriol anti-tobacco lobbyists have for cigarettes is only exceeded by their reaction to anyone who dares question their financial propriety. In 1994, Canadian Member of Parliament John Bryden made that mistake.

Bryden exercised his Parliamentary privileges by asking the Canadian Minister of Revenue to audit the Non-Smoker's Rights Association's charitable arm. Under Canadian law, political lobby groups like the NSRA are not considered charities, and aren't allowed to issue tax receipts for donations. The NSRA wasn't about to stop its lobbying and become non-partisan, but it still wanted taxpayers to subsidize those few private-sector donors it had. (Like most "grassroots" anti-tobacco lobbyists, the NSRA's chief source of funds is government grants.)

Bryden didn't have a particular beef against anti-tobacco lobbyists. Rather he was known for a general campaign against charity scams – people and organizations who claim to be following the government's charity guidelines, but who aren't. Bryden's request to have the NSRA's charitable wing checked for compliance wasn't anything new for him – it was part of a general campaign by the MP to clean up tax evasion and corruption.

Maybe that's why it hit such a nerve with the NSRA.

Garfield Mahood, the NSRA's Executive Director, responded with typically apoplexy. "Bryden's actions are not much different than Richard Nixon's attempt to silence critics," shrieked Mahood.[41] Added Mark Taylor, then president of Physicians for a Smoke-Free Canada: "If Liberal MPs are prepared to harass this organization... MPs like Mr. Bryden may very well be capable of harassing other critics of government policy." Well, we doubt Taylor has anything to hide from a tax law point of view – his lobby group specializes in taking secret gifts from drug companies, not by stretching the definition of a "charity".

CHAPTER EIGHT:
SMOKING AND JUNK SCIENCE

It's virtually impossible to challenge some of the junk science in the war on fun: try telling some do-gooder that Big Macs aren't really that bad, or that second-hand smoke is more of a nuisance than a health problem. Though not one in a thousand busybodies would be able to cite a statistic or study, the talking points have been so well-rehearsed in the media that anyone who denies the conventional wisdom would seem like a flat-earther.

On occasion when contrary studies do come forward to point out that things aren't as apocalyptic as the activists claim they are, those studies are generally ignored – concrete facts are thrown out if they don't support the ideological theory – or they are denounced as propaganda paid for by tobacco or fast food companies.

Curiously, though, many of the sources of anti-smoking "science" are paid for not by neutral universities or academic foundations seeking only the truth, but rather by corporations whose businesses depend on a constant stream of anti-smoking information: pharmaceutical companies who sell smoking cessation.

There's nothing wrong with for-profit pharmaceutical companies paying to promote the idea that cigarettes are unhealthy and their smoking cessation medicines are better – but that's called "advertising" when it's done in other industries. In the anti-smoking industry, though, it's called a scientific journal.

PUBLISHING FOR PROFIT

Take one of the best-respected "academic" journals in the industry, with the anodyne title *Tobacco Control*. This journal presents itself as the very height of academic ethics –

jammed full of footnotes, with contributors a veritable alphabet soup of MDs and PhDs. It calls itself "An international peer review journal for health professionals and others in tobacco control."

But if you look closely at the fine print, you might notice that *Tobacco Control's* editor and other key contributors are all on the payroll – either directly or indirectly – of companies selling anti-smoking meds. Editor Simon Chapman was for years on the payroll of Pharmacia and SmithKlineBeecham (now GlaxoSmithKline), receiving US$3,000 a pop from those companies to talk about quitting smoking. And for years he was a member of an anti-smoking lobby group that received $125,000 annually from Glaxo.[42]

Another Australian on the editorial board of *Tobacco Control*, Melanie Wakefield, is the director of an anti-smoking "research" institute that has received over US$100,000 from Glaxo. Her colleague Ann McNeill didn't just take money; she "has accepted hospitality and on a few occasions, travel costs" from anti-smoking companies, according to a disclosure notice tucked away in *Tobacco Control*.

Receiving bales of cash from companies who have a very direct interest in a particular outcome of "scientific" research is an obvious conflict of interest. But even if there was no financial conflict of interest, almost all of the staff of *Tobacco Control* are directors or members of lobby groups, such as Action on Smoking and Health, which has a political mandate to oppose smoking. In a way, it could be argued that the money from anti-smoking pharmaceutical companies isn't corrupting these "scientists" at all – they had already willingly and publicly admitted their biases by associating with lobby groups. The money paid wasn't going to pre-determine their minds against smoking – they had already made up their minds about what they'd look for long before the pharmaceutical companies cut their cheques. The cheques were more about "thank you" than about "please".

CHAPTER NINE:
WARRIORS AGAINST FUN

So who are the warriors against fun? In Canada, the five-star general of the army would be the aforementioned Garfield Mahood. It's not surprising that Mahood wound up in the anti-smoking business – he spent his early years bouncing around like a public nuisance pinball, engaging in PR and legal stunts that had the distinct flavor of, if not a shake-down artist, a huckster at least. Call him a less-successful, Canadian version of Peter Angelos.

A REBEL LOOKING FOR A CAUSE

As a young man, Mahood channeled his energies to entrepreneurship – promoting a waterskiing show, though it failed; and selling encyclopedias, at which he succeeded. But he soon discovered that there are easier ways to make a name for himself – and money – than to work. As journalist David Olive noted in his book, *Just Rewards*, Mahood combined gonzo stunts, litigation and plain old rudeness long before Michael Moore was on the scene. When Mahood was a student at York University in Toronto, recalls Olive, he once had the inconvenience of having his parked car blocked.[43]

"Leonard Lumbers was one of the first people to discover how prickly the activist can be when crossed," wrote Olive. "Lumbers made the mistake of blocking Mahood's Volvo with his Lincoln in a parking lot at York. Mahood, guessing that the Lincoln could only belong to one of York's big-wig benefactors, hauled Lumbers out of a board of governors meeting and hollered at him in the cold winter night the whole way to the parking lot. When Lumbers, whom Mahood only later discovered was the head of Canada Wire & Cable, refused to apologize for the inconvenience he'd caused, Mahood sued. Mahood let the court date pass, but the story of the student who sued the member of York's board of governors was big news in the campus press and rated a small mention in *The Globe and Mail*."

In some ways it's a fun story – a student showing fearlessness in the face of a "big-wig". (Lumbers was actually a major donor to the university, and a leading force in building its sports teams and facilities.) Asking a big-wig to move isn't unreasonable, and expressing frustration with being blocked in a parking lot – even expressing that rudely – is understandable, too. But where Mahood leaves the realm of the reasonable – and shows his true character – is when he took the step of suing Lumbers. It was obviously a nuisance suit; it would have surely been thrown out of court, with a stern lecture from the judge, warning Mahood against abusing the courts. It showed tenacity and brinkmanship on the part of Mahood – but over the most petty of matters; and it showed an extreme self-righteousness, a willingness to go to absurd lengths just to get the last word. It would be a template that he would follow for years to come.

NUISANCE LAWSUITS

One day Mahood's first wife fell down a staircase when the heel of her shoe fell off. Mahood's wife may have brushed off the incident, but Mahood himself smelled an opportunity to really rub somebody's nose in it – and to make a few bucks in the bargain. According to Olive, "Mahood took the offending footwear back to Eaton's and demanded not only a replacement but a modest compensatory payment. When the department store refused to oblige, Mahood sought opinions from shoe experts in Canada and Britain – including a supporting report unwittingly provided by Eaton's own product-testing lab – and told his story to the papers and CBC radio. Eaton's eventually came up with a new pair of shoes and $200 in damages."

Again, it's not unreasonable to be mad about a broken shoe

– or one's wife's broken shoe. Seeking a replacement isn't unreasonable, either. But what does it say when a person goes to such lengths – calling around internationally to "shoe experts", calling up newspapers and the radio – just for a new pair of shoes and a few dollars? Was it to make a name for himself as a hard-liner who would go to any length, who would actually incur much more costs – in terms of time and expense, than the final award of a new pair of shoes and a few dollars – just to win an argument? And was he – is he – oblivious to how such an absurd and punitive vengeance looks on him?

Even foreign companies were not immune to his approach, according to Olive. "In 1981, Mahood's mother, Evelyn, was bumped from a transatlantic British Airways flight. Mahood, who was seeing his mother off in London, commandeered a phone at the airline's own office and noisily plotted with his Toronto lawyer the lawsuit he planned to bring against Britain's largest air carrier. The airline paid Mahood off with an $850 out-of-court settlement after he threatened to sub-poena enough evidence to fill a small plane."

Being bumped from an airplane isn't rare – and it isn't fun, either for the passenger who's bumped or the besieged air-line workers for whom air rage is now a workplace hazard. Were Mahood to cause such a ruckus in the post 9/11 airport world, he might have wound up spending a night in jail. Not for being upset, but for overreacting so harshly, for marching up to the point of abuse. And what's so odd about it all is that these moments were not dark or embarrassing chapters of his life; they were highlights, moments that he would cel-ebrate, sharing them at the time with the press, or retelling them later as war stories. But a war for what? His own pride and aggrandizement? And against whom? Ordinary employees or companies who make the most trivial of human errors? Mahood positively brags about his bullying, prefacing such tales to author Olive with the words, "And then little old Gar had a great idea..."

THE GRIFTER FINDS HIS CALLING

It was only a matter of time before such a man was attracted to the business of anti-smoking. It had all the hallmarks of the parking lot, the shoe heel and the airline combined – lots of media appeal, big companies to shake down, and plenty of room for lawyers to get in on the action. "I couldn't pick an issue more tailor-made for the type of work I like to do," Mahood said.[44] It sure beats selling encyclopedias.

CHAPTER TEN:
THE INSIDER

Ever since he managed to squeeze a free shoe out of Eaton's, Garfield Mahood has been playing for the cameras. But if there is a media hound who makes Mahood look like a little pup, it's got to be Jeffrey Wigand.

Wigand didn't spend his life in the anti-tobacco trenches like Mahood did. The opposite, in fact – he worked as a vice president for Brown and Williamson, a cigarette company that is now part of R. J. Reynolds. Wigand left Brown and Williamson, and walked over to the "other side": lawyers who were suing tobacco companies. That's why the movie made about him was called *The Insider.*

It was a stunning defection – here was a US$300,000 a year cigarette executive who was willing to tell all of his company's secrets, and right when the lawsuits were piling up against B&W and all the other cigarette companies. It was tailor-made for Hollywood, and it wasn't long before Disney picked up the story, and cast Russell Crowe as Wigand, and Al Pacino as a crusading producer on *60 Minutes* who wanted to blow the lid off the industry.

The movie was a flop – it didn't come close to recouping its budget, and ranked an abysmal 69th place for movies released in 1999.[45] Maybe theatre-goers rebelled against its lecturing, political style. But whatever the reason it failed commercially, *The Insider* failed factually, too.

WHO IS JEFFERY WIGAND?

In the movie, Pacino hollers that Wigand "is the key witness in the biggest public health reform issue in U.S. history." And that's certainly a line that Wigand has repeated – and so have politicians seeking a weapon with which to attack cigarette companies. Allan Rock, when he was Canada's Health Minister, even hired Wigand as an "advisor" and held a Hollywood-style press conference with the subject of the movie in Ottawa. Certainly Ottawa's press gallery seemed happy to run with the script – that Wigand's testimony, and the damning facts about Brown and Williamson that he revealed in a fit of guilt, were enough to take down Big Tobacco, and were essential to a US$246-billion settlement that U.S. cigarette companies agreed to pay over time.

But, in fact, Wigand was not a selfless whistle-blower, putting ethics ahead of self-interest. The anti-smoking movement certainly used him – and the movie – as proof of the moral failings of the cigarette companies. But Wigand, like Mahood, turned out to be more huckster than hero.

Wigand, in the end, was not the "key witness", as Pacino said he was. In fact, he has only testified in a single trial, in Muncie, Indiana[46] – but that was after the movie was already made. The jury that heard Wigand's testimony in Muncie unanimously ruled in favor of the cigarette company, against Wigand's testimony. The centerpiece of *The Insider* – Wigand's testimony at the big trial in Mississippi – was abandoned by Wigand's own lawyers, rather than permit his wobbly testimony to be subject to cross-examination. He wasn't even allowed to finish by his own team.

It is clear that Wigand was not the most important witness in the history of public health. So what was he?

ADDICTED TO FIBBING

He was indeed a vice-president at Brown and Williamson tobacco. But when he came to Canada – to become the government's special advisor – he couldn't quite get his facts straight about his own credentials. His resumé claimed that he received a PhD in biochemistry and endocrinology from the University of Buffalo in 1972. But in an online chat with Canada's *Sun* newspaper chain, he claimed his degree was in biomedical science. And then, in another interview with the *Sun*[47], he said his PhD was in endocrinology.

But the University of Buffalo's Office of Records and Registration denies that Wigand received the medical degrees that he claims, noting that his PhD was in biochemistry – they didn't even offer a PhD in endocrinology when he claimed he earned it.

Does it really matter what Wigand's PhD was in? It should, to the Canadian government that hired him as a special adviser; and it should, to anyone who Wigand and his lawyers ask to take his word over that of his former company. Wigand is a serial nose-stretcher – he once claimed to be on the U.S. Olympic judo team, a fact easily enough proved to be false. [48] Who would tell a fib like that, so easily checked and disproved?

Someone who was desperate to look and sound interesting to TV and movie producers, that's who. Wigand's testimony wasn't particularly useful to the anti-tobacco activists, but his defection itself was exciting – and all the more so if some drama could be added to it. Wigand understood; when he was negotiating his terms with *60 Minutes*, he told them that he had received an anonymous death threat – but not so anonymous that he couldn't conclude that it came from Brown and Williamson.

Of course, alleging a death threat means the police get involved. Edmund Armento, a 27-year veteran of the FBI was assigned to Wigand's complaint. But Armento found fragments of that same threatening letter on Wigand's own computer, and filed an affidavit stating that he felt that Wigand had concocted the "threat" himself, as a hoax to gain sympathy for himself and to put his old bosses in a bad public light.

Wigand had other negative experiences with the law, none of which of course showed up in *The Insider*. Despite his US$300,000 salary, he refused to pay US$325/month support to his wheelchair-bound second wife or their daughter in New York, until they trekked down to a Kentucky court to get the order for four years of arrears. His third wife, Lucretia, didn't fare much better, to the point of having to call the Jefferson County police when a drunk Wigand choked her and struck her face. (Jefferson police later seized a significant number of firearms from the Wigand home). In court, Wigand agreed to six months of "anger control counselling" and continued psychotherapy. But several months later he was wanted by police again for stealing a bottle of Wild Turkey from a Louisville liquor store, pleading guilty to that charge as well.

Wigand's entire public story – and the entire political impact of the movie *The Insider* – is based on a morality play, where Wigand is the innocent, honest man who, after wrestling with his conscience, decides in good faith to blow the whistle on his corrupt, cigarette-making company. In the script, it's Brown and Williamson who breaches the law, by making death threats. In the script, it's Wigand who saves the country in the courts. But none of that's true; Wigand has been in more trials about his own conduct than he has about cigarette-makers' conduct; and the moral exemplar in the movie was in real life a menace to his family and his community. Wigand wasn't hired by the government of Canada for any meaningful advice. He was hired as a PR stunt, to tap into the millions of dollars of goodwill that had been built up by a Disney film. But that movie was a whitewash of Wigand, and a blackening of Brown and Williamson. "I hope we move people with this story. We all took liberties in telling the story to make it more dramatic," Pacino said. That's what this was about – political change. It certainly wasn't a factual documentary. It was a tale, loosely based on the facts. But Wigand – and the mainstream press, and the government of Canada – seemed to believe the Hollywood ending.

A LITTLE BIT OF FICTION

Eric Roth, the man who wrote the script, told the *L.A. Times* that some scenes were invented out of whole cloth simply to "get into the psychology of terror" that Wigand said he felt. Michael Mann, the director, told *The New York Times* that "In the realm of drama, you change everything," which is likely why the film even carries the legal disclaimer that "certain events depicted in the film have been fictionalized for dramatic effect."

Jeffrey Wigand does exist, and he did quit as vice president of a cigarette company. Other than that, *The Insider* is about as factually accurate as a *Star Wars* movie.

CHAPTER ELEVEN:
MAKING FOOD THE NEXT TOBACCO

The war on food isn't as well-developed as the war on smoking – a candy bar executive who was willing to tell all about chocolate likely wouldn't get a big fee from Walt Disney. But that might change.

Take what posed as an investigative report by the CBC.[49] The CBC's Wendy Mesley talked to Dr. Michael Persinger, a scientist at Laurentian University in Sudbury, Ontario, who fed his rats sugar water one week, and regular water the next, and found out that rats prefer sugar water. So far, so obvious.

"These rats and we humans are very similar when it comes to our brains and our behaviour," cooed Mesley. Actually, rats don't have such gifts as common sense, reason, self-discipline, or even plain old guilt.

Perhaps sensing that the elementary-school-style science fair project with hamsters and sugar didn't quite make the case that we are all just rats in a big terrarium controlled by Big Sugar, Mesley interviewed a fat teenager. "When I want something good to eat, I'll, like, have it," Jonathan Loza said to Mesley. Just like the rats.

Mesley sensed she had some convincing to do – maybe her chubby teenager just needed to exercise more, and eat his veggies. "But it's hard," she said. "Look at what he and most suburban kids are up against these days." Mesley and the rest of the government-paid CBC team walked back and forth within a three kilometer radius of young Jonathan, and found 92 fast food signs. Not a lot, considering most Canadian towns would fit into a three kilometer radius. "Many of those ads are aimed at the most susceptible – the young. Young people like Jonathan," said Mesley.

Naturally, being a government-owned TV station, CBC's

first instinct was to ask other government bureaucrats to intervene. "The first step is let's understand the issue," said Mary Bush of Health Canada, not quite the condemnation of restaurants that Mesley was hoping for. "But if the food industry's getting richer, and we all are all hooked on eating French fries and candy...?" replied Mesley, hopefully. Those rich food industrialists! They've hooked young Jonathan!

"Back at the food court, it all comes down to you and me," concluded Mesley. "Or, are the scientists right – that we don't have as much choice as we like to think?" There's no doubt where the CBC stands.

TEACHING IRRESPONSIBILITY

Last word went to the rat scientist. "If your culture has taught you do so something, really there is no voluntarism involved." He was introduced as a rat scientist, measuring whether or not rats like sugar better than water. Over the course of the show, he apparently became a human sociologist, concluding that the sugar "culture" has "taught" Jonathan so well that he is no longer responsible for himself. And you think these fearmongers will stop at tobacco?

USING THE TOBACCO LAWSUIT TEMPLATE

John Banzhaf didn't. He's a U.S. lawyer who cut his teeth going after the tobacco companies. Now he's turning to the greener pastures of food – and using the same arguments. "I think when a fast food company deliberately doesn't tell you important information, that both legally and morally they bear some responsibility," he says, building up the image of evil, lying corporate cooks, just like tobacco executives but in chefs hats.[50] Eric Schlosser, author of *Fast Food Nation*, borrows the same anti-tobacco trope used by Mesley – that food companies prey on kids. "One of the things I want to do is put pressure on these companies, not to go out of business but to change what they're marketing to kids."[51]

GST – GOODIES AND SWEETS TAX

And if the attacks are the same as in the tobacco wars, so are the prescriptions – including taxes on fatty food. John Schaafsma, a Canadian health economics professor, argues that "by taxing fat, you're really killing two birds with one stone. You're raising tax revenue for the health care system. At the same time, you're discouraging the consumption of fat."[52]

Some doctors disagree, including weight management Dr. Robert Dent. "This is a medical problem, we don't tax salt for our patients with hypertension, why should we be taxing fat to try and prevent overweight?"[53] Allan Rock, the Canadian health minister when the fat tax idea was first bruited, didn't rule out the idea. "Some countries have tried a Twinkie tax. I guess we're waiting to see if it does any good. Obviously what works is what we're interested in. I'm just not sure the long arm of the government reaching through taxes is always the answer."[54] That never stopped Rock from jacking up tobacco taxes.

SO THIS VEGAN WALKS INTO MCDONALD'S...

As with the war on tobacco, the food lawsuits have begun. Harjinder Khant, was one of six Vancouver plaintiffs suing McDonald's – a restaurant built on meat – for using beef tallow in its fries. Khant's case: he's a sensitive vegetarian, though apparently not sensitive enough to keep out of McDonald's restaurants. "Nobody told me there's beef in the fries. So when I heard it, I was totally outraged, and totally shocked."[55] Khant's lawyer, Harish Bahrti, claimed McDonald's deceived his client by being deceptively vegetarian in its appearance. "That is exactly what the intent of the law is, to protect the consumer from deceptive business practices."

But McDonald's didn't deceive Khant, or any other "vegetarians" who thought that McDonald's would be a good place to find meat-free food. Because every single McDonald's outlet has a detailed nutrition brochure listing ingredients – including the beef fat used to make their fries so tasty. Could it be – just possibly, maybe – that Bahrti deceived himself to indulge his tastebuds? And that maybe he, as an allegedly devout vegetarian, should have used a little bit more common sense, as a vegetarian, than to eat at the house that Ronald McDonald built?

Outrageous, snaps Bahrti. After all, he claims he asked the teenaged McDonald's clerk for her opinion on the matter, not wanting to trouble himself with reading the facts. It's what lawyers call plausible deniability. "I asked them, these guys, 'this is vegetarian?' They said 'yes, this is vegetarian, potato fries', but they didn't tell, they didn't tell anyone."

At least they didn't the CBC rat scientist's "society told me to do it" excuse.

CHAPTER TWELVE:
WAPPEL'S WHOPPER

In Canada, the attack against food has come mainly from politicians and lobbyists, not lawyers. One proposed law introduced by Tom Wappel, a Member of Parliament from Winnipeg, would require extreme and costly labeling of foods by any groceries and restaurants bigger than a mom and pop operation.

Called C-398, Wappel's bill would change grocers and restaurateurs from customer-oriented retailers into government-oriented rule-followers. Red meat would take a back seat to red tape.[56] C-398 requires any "meat, poultry or seafood" sold in Canada to have a label listing "the number of calories and the amount of total fat, saturated fat, trans fat, cholesterol, sodium, total carbohydrate, dietary fibre, sugars, protein, iron, calcium, vitamin A and vitamin C" on each piece of fish or meat sold.

That applies to a butcher carving you meat to order; to a fisherman at a fish market, selling you a catch right off his boat; to farmers at a farmers market. Anyone who sells more than a token minimum (it wouldn't apply to church bake sales, for instance) would be required to label every piece of food sold.

NEWSPAPER-SIZED MENUS

And heaven forbid you happen to own a restaurant. Any printed menu would be required to list, for each item, the number of calories, sodium and the sum of saturated fat plus trans fat – right on the menu. Restaurants that didn't have menus – for example, drive-thrus – would not be exempt. They would still have to publish the calorie count for each item, right on their big menu boards. And vending machines would have to comply– even if it meant changing the vending machine signage every time a different item was stocked in the machine.

You'd think that would be onerous enough – labeling every item of food sold in the country. But C-398 comes with a whole extra set of rules restricting how foods are marketed – and even what pictures can be on food labeling. Section 5.3(1) of the bill would require that, anytime an ingredient "is emphasized by words or pictures on the label," that ingredient must be listed as a percentage of weight. So milk bottles with pictures of cows on them will now have to be labeled for the percentage of each bottle made up of cows. Chicken of the Sea tuna will have to indicate that it actually doesn't contain any chicken.

And don't think that these onerous labeling requirements could be dealt with by using legal-style fine print. After all, the whole point of laws like C-398 is to label consumer items to get the government's message out, not the food manufacturer's message, or messages that consumers actually want. So section 5.3(2) requires that whenever an ingredient is emphasized by words or pictures, the labeled ingredient must be "in characters at least 50 percent the size of those employed in the common name of the food." So Chicken of the Sea must now print "Chicken, 0% by weight" at least half as large as the brand name.

PRIVATE FOOD REGULATION – A MODEL

Is there another way to satisfy that sector of society that demands such detailed information about their food – but doesn't burden food producers and retailers, or the millions of consumers who aren't that finicky?

The answer to this modern question may come from a surprisingly ancient example: kosher food.

Consumers who strictly follow Judaism's dietary laws need to know that food products are kosher – the word for "fit" or "acceptable" in Hebrew. Of course, what's tested is not calories or fat, but adherence to religious rules ranging from prohibitions against mixing milk with meat to the precise and humane method of slaughtering animals.

What is the same, though, is the niche demand for very specialized – and often expensive – certification and labeling of food. And, with the exception of New York State's anachronistic government-run kosher certification, North America and indeed most of the world is governed by private, competing kosher certification agencies.

Kosher certification, in fact, is so common that most consumers probably buy kosher-certified products without even knowing it. In food products ranging from Coca-Cola to Heinz Ketchup to Alpha-Bits cereal, these religious food standards are met. Different kosher consumers have different standards of strictness that they demand in their certification. Some products feature an "MK"—meaning they've been certified by rabbis in Montreal; others might favor a national certification symbol, such as the ubiquitous OU symbol. Food manufacturers seek out kosher certification to please their customers. They bear the symbols on their labels to communicate to a whole segment of observant Jewish consumers that their products meet their needs – consumers who might otherwise not buy them. That's what food makers do best: they market their products to meet the needs and desires of consumers. And they've been doing it all along without the help of politicians like Tom Wappel.

CHAPTER THIRTEEN:
MR. GROSS-OUT MAKES A
"DOCUMENTARY"

If food is to fall like tobacco did, it's got to be denormalized. The first big attack on fast food's normal place in popular culture came in the form of the 2004 movie, *Super Size Me*, by gross-out filmmaker Morgan Spurlock. In the movie – styled as a documentary – Spurlock goes on an all-McDonald's diet for a month. He must eat at that restaurant morning, noon and night, and whenever he is offered a "super size" portion, he must accept.

TV'S SHLOCK JOCK

Spurlock first made a name for himself as the director and star of *I Bet You Will*, an Internet TV show that MTV later picked up. The theme of *I Bet You Will* was pretty simple: Spurlock paid people money to see what kind of disgusting things they'd do on tape for a few bucks – a precursor to the gross-out challenges on TV's *Fear Factor*.

Spurlock's fetish was eating gross things, or at least eating gross amounts of things. In one episode of *I Bet You Will*, he paid someone $235 to eat a giant jar of mustard on video. In another, he paid a woman $250 to eat three sticks of butter with her own hair mixed in.

It wasn't just the money, though: Spurlock's co-host said "I can get people to do it for free, just because they're on MTV. They don't care. People are crazy."[57] But *I Bet You Will* never claimed to be a documentary; *Super Size Me* does.

Spurlock does for the nutrition debate what Michael Moore does for politics – he acts as an incendiary troublemaker who never lets the facts get in the way of scoring a few points and selling a few more tickets. He's not a documentary filmmaker as much as a jester; *Super Size Me* was no more a serious investigation into North American health than *I Bet You Will* was.

CONFLICTS OF INTEREST

If *Super Size Me* were scrutinized the same way Spurlock would scrutinize a movie promoting hamburgers, it would be torn to shreds for its conflicts of interest. Spurlock's wife is a vegan chef whose business is flogged not just on the movie's website and credits, but in the actual movie itself. And Natural Ovens Bakery, which lobbies to get school lunch contracts, receives promotional consideration in the film's credits, and is featured as a kind of anti-fast-food hero in the film. That's what consumer advocates would call "product placement" – when money-making corporations ensure that they just happen to show up in a movie in a positive light. For Spurlock, *Super Size Me* wasn't just a chance to rant, it was a chance to do some subliminal advertising for his businesses run by his wife and friends. How fitting that Spurlock's production company is called "The Con."

A TRIAL LAWYER PRODUCTION

But that ethical lapse pales next to Spurlock's decision to contract out editorial direction of his movie to John Banzhaf, the health "expert" used by trial lawyers to quarterback litigation against tobacco companies.

Banzhaf was the health law strategist who destroyed the concept of personal responsibility when it came to smoking – and helped secure trial lawyers more than a quarter of a trillion dollars in winnings from tobacco companies. Now he's set his sights on suing food companies, and Spurlock was more than willing to let Banzhaf steer his film.

Banzhaf has perfected a legal strategy for taking on companies that have traditionally been seen as harmless, normal companies – as cigarette manufacturers once were. Banzhaf managed to convince a few juries that smoking wasn't just a habit – it was a full-out addiction that no reasonable person could ever escape. Tobacco wasn't simply something that

69

everybody knew wasn't healthy – it was diabolically unhealthy, and because cigarette companies didn't fully disclose everything they knew about it, smokers couldn't be responsible for their own actions despite what they knew. According to Banzhaf, cigarette companies trap and manipulate smokers like marionettes, especially children. Under Banzhaf's direction, Spurlock made all these points against fast food companies, too.

The word "addiction" is used by Spurlock dozens of times in *Super Size Me* – and he even claims that he himself became addicted to McDonald's food, that he was irritable until he got his daily fix. That claim made for a dramatic moment, just like when on his TV show he paid a girl $250 to eat sticks of butter with her own hair mashed in. The claim falls apart on the slightest scrutiny – Spurlock is shown easily and happily moving back to his wife's veggie cooking after the movie's experiment is over; no addict's hankering for a Big Mac there. But how many thousands of movie-watchers – and prospective jurors in the tobacco-style fat lawsuits of the years to come – now believe with their own eyes that McDonald's is addictive?

POISONING THE JURY POOL

Banzhaf knows exactly what he's doing – he's shaping the battlefield now, laying down layers of sediment for when the lawsuits start. He even appears in the movie, quoting himself as it were. "In terms of responsibility it's fair to point the big gun at McDonald's," he says, in case anyone was wondering who the first deep-pocketed plaintiff would be. Why not start with the biggest bank account? After bringing down big tobacco, Big Macs must seem like easy pickings.

One of Banzhaf's strategies from the cigarette lawsuits was to demonize tobacco companies, to always refer to them as criminal organizations, run by immoral men. It's hard to believe, but cigarette companies were once the most highly respected companies in America; many of the men who signed the Declaration of Independence farmed it. They have been successfully denormalized; food companies are next.

McDonald's doesn't merely advertise, claims Banzhaf. It "lures in young children." Responsible people market. Child molesters – predators – "lure". Banzhaf knows what he's doing with his language.

"You've *got* to take your kid there," he says – parents don't have a choice. With the McDonald's playrooms, claims Banzhaf, parents aren't able to resist their pleading kids who want to go. It's not a matter of personal choice, even for parents. It's about corporate executives "luring" children, and parents unable to resist.

You can tell that the legal brief has already been written, as Banzhaf recites the ways that tobacco companies, er, McDonald's, target kids: playgrounds, birthday parties, kids' Happy Meals with toys, and of course a child-friendly clown, Ronald McDonald.

IT'S ABOUT THE MONEY

Banzhaf and Spurlock claim they care about kids – more, even, than kids' own parents care about them. But they also interview Samuel Hirsch, another anti-McDonald's lawyer. He's less shy about his motivations. Asked why he's filed lawsuits against fast food restaurants, he answers "you mean motives besides the monetary compensation? You want to hear a noble cause, is that it?" It's a rare flash of what the anti-hamburger lobby is really about – tobacco-style cash payouts to lawyers. Kids are just the tear-jerking excuses to get at the corporate treasuries. Spurlock must have forgotten to edit that part out.

It's a huge task to rebrand an entire industry as quasi-criminal – and it's certainly an audacious one. It's shocking to hear the first time – but by the millionth time it's repeated, it's conventional wisdom. Cigarettes were once an accept-able personal choice, just like drinking beer or wine is. Not any longer – a million repetitions of Banzhaf-style denunci-ations have turned radical ideas into the commonplace. That's Spurlock's job – and right now, only gross-out TV jesters and voracious trial lawyers might be up to it. But they're just the sharp point on the end of the spear. And oth-ers with a personal or economic interest aren't hard to find.

Paul Stitt, whose Natural Ovens Bakery receives promo-tional consideration from Spurlock's movie, is more than willing to chime in: McDonald's "want to be there to addict kids for life." So schools should ban burgers, and hire his company.

Spurlock's wife, whose catering company is featured in the movie, knows her lines. Eating meat, she says, is "a system that is corrupt and immoral and wrong and hurtful." That would be quite a sweeping statement for a deep-thinking philosopher to make, let alone a ditzy young vegan chef to make, but somebody had to say it.

Spurlock himself tried hard to come across as the neutral investigator – a real documentary filmmaker, not an agent provocateur. But, true to his *I Bet You Will* roots, he couldn't resist the most exciting scene in the film, when he forced himself to vomit up his Big Mac on film. It won't win any Oscars for best Actor, but it certainly drove home Banzhaf's point: fast food is poisonous.

CHAPTER FOURTEEN:
THE DEMONIZATION OF HAMBURGERS

Spurlock's film had some particularly incendiary footage, some of which was mercifully cut from the theatre version, but which was added to its DVD release. One such scene was an interview with Eric Schlosser, the author of *Fast Food Nation*, another calumny against fast food.

Schlosser agreed with Spurlock's wife that beef production was a "cruel, cruel system." Fast food wasn't just unhealthy, or a choice that could be made in moderation; it is "food poisoning", and damages the environment. It increases homelessness, and hurts people in the Third World. If tobacco executives were bad, food executives were positively diabolical. Just in case he wasn't clear, Schlosser called McDonald's and other restaurant giants "mean, greedy companies." And if *that* wasn't clear enough Schlosser said that McDonald's achievement of having one common taste, worldwide at all of their outlets, was as slogan "that's like *sieg heil*." Even cigarette makers haven't been called Nazis.

Spurlock was delighted with Schlosser's rant – and Banzhaf, Hirsch and the other lawyers, no longer on screen, must have been, too. Ronald McDonald, by appealing to children, was "insidious", said Schlosser. In case viewers couldn't get the point, Spurlock prompted him further: "Is Ronald McDonald comparable to Joe Camel?" he asked, comparing it, Banzhaf-style, to the now-retired cartoon camel allegedly used to draw children to cigarettes.

BURGERS: THE ROOT OF ALL EVIL

Schlosser and Spurlock then go on a bit of a round-house rant – alleging that fast food companies treat their employees badly, artificially keep sugar prices cheap to hook children; abuse foreign workers, including the Chinese workers who make the toys for Happy Meals; crack down on unions, and, bizarrely, that McDonald's even deploys corporate spies to undermine Greenpeace activists – by sleeping with them. No urban legend or conspiracy theory is too nutty for these two; and while such arguments might not make it in a court of law, there's no defence lawyer in the theatres to object to the junk science and junk economics being offered up as fact. Whichever of the arguments lobbed up by these two McDonald's-haters sticks, doesn't matter – as long as one of them sticks, and sticks long enough to accompany a potential juror into the coming trial of the century.

CHAPTER FIFTEEN:
THE WAR ON SUVS

Tobacco companies were pretty big game for the trial lawyers, politicians and public health advocates to hunt. Food companies and restaurants are even bigger. But perhaps nothing makes a trial lawyer lick his lips more than the prospect of bringing down the auto industry. Welcome to the biggest battle of all in the war on fun: the fight against SUVs.

At first glance, the war against SUVs sounds too fanciful even for the most wild-eyed lawyer. Like food, transportation is essential to life, a claim that tobacco couldn't make. And even the rickety logic used in the anti-McDonald's lawsuits wouldn't work against cars – there is no automobile equivalent to eating too much fast food.

But the war on fun isn't fueled by logic or science; it runs on activists' feelings of moral superiority, politicians' desire for headlines and lawyers' desire for big paydays. Against those enemies, even mighty Henry Ford would tremble.

Like tobacco and food, the war against SUVs requires that the battlefield be prepared – which means the North American love affair with driving had to be checked. That's a tough battle, when getting a first car is a rite of passage for teenagers and the open road is a metaphor for freedom. Let cramped Europeans and Japanese ride on trains – for us, it's the liberty to come and go when we please, where we please.

HOLLYWOOD HYPOCRITES

Vehicles are a pretty central part of popular culture to attack; so who better to call upon than Hollywood moguls like Larry David, producer of TV's *Seinfeld* and his wife Laurie David, and Lawrence Bender, producer of hit movies like *Pulp Fiction* and *Good Will Hunting*. Together with political gadfly Arianna Huffington and other well-heeled do-gooders and headline seekers, they set up a lobby group with the specific goal of demonizing SUVs. Though they all hail from the tonier neighborhoods of Los Angeles, they dubbed themselves the Detroit Project. It wasn't just an attempt to make their champagne and caviar club seem more working class. It was also an attempt to start defining an enemy for the public to blame – big, bad SUV companies. Like the wars against cigarettes and food, ordinary drivers – moms and dads taking their kids to soccer, or bringing home some furniture from IKEA. The enemy had to be someone else – in this case automobile companies who "refused" to make smaller cars.

The Detroit Project was little more than a website and a few self-obsessed celebrities – their splashy debut happened to coincide with the release of Huffington's new book; shortly thereafter she ran an ill-fated campaign for California governor (against Arnold Schwarzenegger, practically synonymous with the Hummer SUV).

The Detroit Project wasn't much of a project; its slick website had lengthy, gushing biographies of the four celebrities who "founded" it, and a very prominent donations page. But the real action was three TV ads utterly devoid of science or logic – but chock full of vitriol for SUVs. To call the ads shocking is to state the obvious; but that's the point. When you're taking on something as all-American as an SUV, any criticism is going to sound jarring. The Hollywood wizards knew that, and opted to go big – may as well equate driving a Ford Explorer or a pickup truck with, oh, Saddam Hussein and Osama bin Laden. In for a dime, in for a dollar.

"I HELPED HIJACK AN AIRPLANE"

One ad featured SUV "owners" confessing to their sins. "I helped hijack an airplane," said one, in an ad aired shortly after 9/11. Classy stuff, that Arianna. "I helped blow up a nightclub," said another actor. "I helped our enemies develop weapons of mass destruction." "I sent our soldiers off to war."

Two other ads helped paint the ideological picture. One claimed that there is a dream car out there that "gets 40 miles to every gallon . . . the only problem is Detroit won't build it." Yes, just like the CIA has secretly discovered the cure for cancer but "won't" release it, Detroit is part of some secret conspiracy, rounded out by a third ad, featuring a man in CIA-style sunglasses – an "oil company executive" whose money goes to "terrorists" – while showing al Qaeda thugs on the screen.

In that sense, the opening shot on the war on SUVs was identical to the *Super Size Me* war on food – a shocking blow to an integral part of our daily lives, so outrageous, so baseless, that most TV viewers would be utterly unprepared for it. It is an emotional wallop, not an intellectual argument, but that's what this was about: stripping off the veneer of normalcy of a very normal activity, and comparing it to supporting terrorism. It's insane, actually; but a big lie usually works better than a lot of little lies.

What would motivate this propaganda? The personal vanity of the Detroit Project's co-founders cannot be underestimated. Huffington has made a career out of being a political shock jock; Laurie David is the bored Hollywood wife of a producer famous for vacuous, if funny TV – her rich girl dalliances into environmental radicalism give her an intellectual gloss and a moral authority that being a lady who lunches never could.

CHAPTER SIXTEEN:
THE MEDIA PUPPETMASTER

The fact that all four of the co-founders of the Detroit Project indulge in the materialist consumption that would make Liberace blush is hard to ignore when they're playing TV ads accusing drivers of morally supporting terror. It's a touch rich for Huffington, who regularly flies around the country on private jets, to complain about the few extra gallons of gas needed to power an SUV.[58] Anyone with an air-conditioned 9,000 square foot mansion in Brentwood who calls for energy efficiency is open to charges of having other political motivations at heart.

Those motivations might be found by looking at the advertising agency that produced the Detroit Project's ads: Fenton Communications. The Detroit Project claims to be an aw-shucks group of regular folks concerned about SUVs – even if they are all Hollywood millionaires. Fenton Communications, though, is one of North America's toughest campaigners for every aspect of the war on fun. Named after its founder, David Fenton, the firm handles public relations for every big leftist organization out there, from Greenpeace to radio's Air America to Huffington's own campaign for governor.

So the Detroit Project is just one more tentacle in the octopus of leftist groups. That's no crime (though the United Auto Workers union, whose jobs depend on Detroit, might want to have a word with the folks at Fenton, which handles their account, too). But perhaps the real secret to the SUV smear comes from the deadliest and richest of Fenton's clients: The American Trial Lawyers Association.

As with tobacco and food, trial lawyers need a sympathetic jury if they're going to bag themselves prey as big as General Motors. Take an SUV company to trial today, and even the late Johnnie Cochran would be laughed out of the courthouse – North Americans are just not ready to turn on that industry yet. But spend a few million dollars on ads that demonize SUVs – and emphasize to jurors that they aren't responsible for the purported faults of the SUVs they drive; evil auto and oil executives are, "Detroit" is – and you might just win a verdict one day. Of course, it's against the law to tamper with a jury once it's been selected. But there are no SUV trials on now, and there might not be for a few years. So why not tamper with the whole jury pool now – by running ads equating car and oil companies with terrorists?

THE ALAR SCARE BUSINESS MODEL

It's an extreme argument, which is why David Fenton is just the guy to make it. He first made his bones in the radical anti-nuclear movement (which raises the question: if oil is out, and nuclear power if out, what exactly are we supposed to use as fuel?). But his real break came in 1989, when he orchestrated a nation-wide panic over Alar, a preservative used to keep apples fresh. Fenton leaked a false memo on Alar to CBS news' *60 Minutes*, suggesting that Alar was linked to cancer, especially in kids. The crew at *60 Minutes* ran big with the story, causing a national health scare and Alar's removal from the market.[59]

Except that in reality, Alar isn't harmful at all. Fenton was whipping up public concerns – and using the media to do the heavy lifting for him – for the benefit of his client, the Natural Resources Defence Council, an environmental group (which is prominently featured on the Detroit Project's website). Fenton was so pleased with himself that he bragged about it to other clients. "We designed [the Alar campaign] so that revenue would flow back to the Natural Resources Defense Council from the public," he wrote in a memo. "And we sold this book about pesticides through a 900 number and the 'Donahue Show.' And to date there has been $700,000 in net revenue from it... A modest investment repaid itself many-fold in tremendous media exposure and substantial, immediate revenue," Fenton bragged. "Lines started forming in health food stores. The sales of organic produce soared. All of which we were very happy about."

SURPRISE – TRIAL LAWYERS

Now, blackening the name of SUVs isn't going to help the sales of organic produce, and it's not going to help the cause of Fenton's autoworker clients. It did propel Huffington's name into the papers for her book launch and her political campaign. But no one benefited more from Fenton's demonization of SUVs than his other clients – the trial lawyers. Like the Alar scare, Fenton didn't actually have to spend a lot of money promoting the idea – he gave it to CBS that ran with it at their own financial expense, and using their own credibility. So, too, with the Detroit Project. It's unclear just how often the SUVs-equals-terrorism ads actually ran on television as paid spots, but, like Alar, the media buzz sparked by such inflammatory ads was the whole point. So far, automakers haven't surrendered the way Alar and the apple growers did. They're not done yet, but then again neither is Fenton.

Meanwhile, Fenton's keeping busy with other projects. When Dana Reeve, the widow of Superman actor Christopher Reeve, announced recently that she had lung cancer, Fenton jumped into action in the war against smoking. Fenton worked his media relations magic and helped his client, the American Lung Association, boost membership in an online anti-smoking campaign by 50%.[60] Consider it a minor detail that Reeve was not a smoker.[61]

A guru like Fenton knows that the war against SUVs can't come from the Hollywood elite alone – that's enough to build buzz with celebrity-obsessed journalists and stargazers. But what about Middle America, "red state" families who regard the idea of Hollywood morality as an oxymoron? Fenton's got that angle covered, too. He's the brains behind an environmental front called the Evangelical Environmental Network.[62]

ENVIRONMENTALISM AS A RELIGION

You've probably never heard of the Evangelical Environmental Network; they're not a church, and, like the Detroit Project, they're not a large grassroots "network". But they did come up with a catchy slogan that you probably have heard of: "What Would Jesus Drive?"

Like the Detroit Project, like the Alar scare, Fenton harnessed the power and resources of the media to do his heavy lifting for him. A Google search shows more than 91,000 websites answer to that query, and 32,000 more for the Detroit Project, with more every day. Like the Alar scare, Fenton couldn't help but to brag about how he snookered the media with the Jesus campaign. The campaign "was like a gift from heaven," the company boasted in a memo to their clients.[63] Fenton told how they spent just a handful of dollars running the ad in paid markets, but made the ad available for free to the news media. They "did turn an initial investment of just under $70,000 into $3-4 million's worth of free media," gushed Fenton.

That kind of showy salesmanship, using Christianity as a political brand, didn't sit well with more established Christian groups. After the Evangelical Environmental Network's noisy invocation of Jesus' name, Thomas Mason of Focus on the Family, an established Christian organization, wrote to an EEN advocate to point out not only the theologically foolish nature of the question "What Would Jesus Drive?", but also that Christians actually do believe in other things – as did Jesus himself – and that "I am not sure that either air pollution or petroleum reserves in any way match these other issues." Mason had seen enough hustler televangelists to know a phoney when he saw one. "I hope that your commitment... to correcting the moral freefall in our society runs as deep as the commitment to improving the environment," he wrote to EEN.[64]

The funny thing is, we actually know what Jesus would drive. According to the Bible, he rode a donkey – hardly an environmentally sound alternative to an automobile, and needless to say less practical in today's world. But the point wasn't meant to be sensible – just like Fenton's comparison of driving an SUV with supporting terrorism. It was meant to imply that driving an SUV is immoral, something that good Christians wouldn't do, just like the Detroit Project was meant to say that American patriots shouldn't drive terror-loving SUVs. The slogan was meant to startle with its cheekiness, not to persuade through logic. And, as Fenton turned up the volume knob on his campaigns, the more radical Earth Liberation Front was right behind, with a series of crime sprees, vandalizing and in some cases even torching SUVs and car dealerships across America.[65] Call it a good cop-bad cop routine.

CHAPTER SEVENTEEN:
PORSCHE DRIVERS VS. SUV DRIVERS

Next to Fenton's front groups, the greatest demonizer of SUVs would undoubtedly be Keith Bradsher, the author of the bestselling book *High and Mighty – SUVs: The World's Most Dangerous Vehicles and How They Got That Way.* The title pretty much gives it away; that 441-page door-stopper goes so far as to call for juries to send "prosperous families... to prison for manslaughter after a deadly crash if they were in an SUV they did not need."[66] Normally, sending entire families to prison requires a greater crime than just "choosing the Suburban over the minivan," but Bradsher practically longs for such a verdict. And he's thinking like a trial lawyer: "This is unlikely to happen, however, until public perceptions of SUVs change enough that juries look askance at anyone who causes a death or serious injury while driving an SUV for a trip that could have been made in a car. That day is probably a long way off," he writes. You can hear the disappointment as he realizes that most people don't yet share his vengeance. But now that *High and Mighty* was published, you can bet that day is getting nearer.

ANTI-SUV SNOBBERY

Some of *High and Mighty* is an attempt to prove that SUVs are more dangerous and less fuel efficient. But much of the book is in the Huffington vein – an attempt to personally demonize people associated with SUVs – those who make them, sell them or drive them. "Who has been buying SUVs since automakers turned them into family vehicles?" asks Bradsher. "They tend to be people who are insecure and vain," he writes. "Above all, they are apt to be self-centered and self-absorbed."[67] Thirty million North Americans have bought SUVs. Is Bradsher's pathologizing of them any more credible because it's written in a book by a journalist, instead of uttered by a preening celebrity in Hollywood? Surely there is a more persuasive criticism of SUVs than plain old name-calling?

Perhaps its what psychologists call projection; in the book, Bradsher praises a European car enthusiast who buys both a Rolls Royce and a Porsche.[68] Surely the owner of a Rolls can more credibly be called vain than a driver of a Ford Explorer; surely a driver of a two-seat Porsche is more accurately called self-absorbed than a mom loading up a Lincoln Navigator with kids. But then again, flying in private jets didn't stop Huffington from complaining about SUVs' fuel efficiency.

What is so telling about the war on SUVs – and what gives it a striking similarity with the war against smoking and the war against food – is that it is so classist, so anti-middle class. The war against smoking is not really against smoking in general; it's against smoking cigarettes – expensive, classy cigars have retained their chic. The war against food is against McDonald's – a place the opinion aristocracy would never go. It is not against premium priced Ben and Jerry's ice cream, or fine French pastries. And the snobbery of Bradsher – and his Hollywood buddies – is just as obvious. Two of his large (if unfounded) criticisms of SUVs is that they have poor fuel efficiency and that they are more dangerous – or, at least, are driven more dangerously. How can such a critic turn around and admire someone who drives a gas-guzzling, racecar like a Porsche?

But that's the difference; a Porsche is sophisticated. It's driven by the kind of people with whom Bradsher, a *New York Times* journalist, associates. His kind of people don't drive SUVs; that's far too common. That's what seems to bother Bradsher; SUVs are just far too plentiful – they are not special. Huffington herself gives the game away, when talking about selling her SUV and Lexus to buy an eco-friendly

Toyota Prius hybrid. She was out on the town: "The parking lot was full of Jaguars and Bentleys," she said, "and my host brought everyone out to the driveway to look at Arianna's car. It became this point of attraction." This is about style, you see; anyone with money can have a Jaguar. Buying a Prius showed that she had both money and taste. But then you knew that; who else would refer to herself in the third person – everyone wanted to look "at Arianna's car".

It's true that both Bradsher's admired Porsche and an SUV use more gas than does a regular car. The Porsche's excuse is that it's a sports car, which seems to satisfy Bradsher. SUVs burn more gas because they're bigger. Bradsher thinks that families who use bigger cars when a smaller one would do should face prison if they cause an accident; but not everyone lives in Bradsher's world of different cars for different moods. Moms who take their kids to hockey in an SUV probably use the same vehicle when running an errand alone – that's just economic reality. The economic snobbery shown by Bradsher and his fabulous friends smacks of the kind of derision shown by so many elites towards Wal-Mart – not that Wal-Mart is execrable, but that the very thought of being seen there would make one a pariah in finer social circles. You can practically hear the fake mid-Atlantic accent kicking in as Bradsher writes about SUV owners: "they are frequently nervous about their marriages and uncomfortable about parenthood."[69] You just know his editor had to delete the words "unlike my friends and I" after that jab. Who's really the self-conscious one here?

JUNK SCIENCE ABOUT SUV SAFETY

Bradsher does have some criticisms of SUVs that do not involve personal insults. He claims that SUVs are more dangerous – to their own passengers, in that they roll over more frequently than regular cars, and to other cars that the SUVs might hit. He claims that they guzzle more fuel than regular cars, and that they have greater environmental emissions. This is as close as it gets to a scientific attack on SUVs; but, as with the war on smoke and food, it's a mixture of junk science and just plain fibbing.

SUVs are higher than cars, and have a higher center of gravity – so their rollover rate is higher than regular cars, which can roll over too. But rollovers are one of the rarest events in a car accident – happening in just 2.5% of all motor vehicle crashes. In the other 97.5% of accidents – front, side and rear impacts – SUVs perform better than regular cars. According to the U.S. National Highway Traffic Safety Authority, the fatality rate for those accidents is 157 per million vehicles for a small car, but just 62 per million for SUVs – making SUVs more than twice as safe. When all kinds of crashes are combined, including rare rollovers, SUVs are still measurably safer, with 160 fatalities per million vehicles, as opposed to 208 per million for small cars and 164 per million for medium cars. Large cars and pickup trucks slightly edge out SUVs at 134 and 135 fatalities per million vehicles respectively[70] – but Fenton tell us that Jesus isn't likely to be driving a Lincoln Town Car.

The fact is, all cars are getting safer, and traffic fatalities are the lowest in memory. From 1980 to 2000, traffic fatalities for all cars have declined by 49% when measured on a per vehicle basis. But SUV safety has been even more impressive, with a 73% reduction in fatalities. Critics would say that even if SUVs are safe for their own passengers, they endanger others on the road – that's the "crime" Bradsher wants to send families to "prison" for. This isn't a new issue, though. After the oil shock of 1973, and with the new wave of Japanese imports, the majority of new cars on North American roads were dramatically smaller than the big gas-guzzlers before them. Today's Hummers look pretty big, but only 40% of vehicles these days weigh more than two tons. In 1975, that figure was 65%. Even with the popularity of

SUVs, there are fewer big vehicles on the road now than 30 years ago.

It's true that compact cars are more vulnerable in accidents with big SUVs than if they hit another Mini Cooper; and even a Lincoln Navigator is going to have problems if it collides with a bus. As long as the highways are shared by vehicles of different sizes, that's a factor. But it's not a big factor – according to a study by the Insurance Institute for Highway Safety,[71] collisions between cars and SUVs or pickups account for about 15% of all occupant deaths. That figure rises only to 16% for the very lightest cars getting into crashes with SUVs. The horror scenario – a car that's smaller than normal getting into a crash with the largest SUV – was the cause of only 1% of all small car accident deaths in the U.S. in 1997, or 136 out of 12,144.[72]

CHAPTER EIGHTEEN: COMPARING POLLUTION

Complaining that little cars are little isn't the main gist of the anti-SUV attacks. Very few people will buy the implication that Bradsher makes about SUV drivers: that they are emotionally insecure people who recklessly endanger their neighbors on the highways and therefore deserve prison. That's the criticism that may yield the big payouts in court one day, if a lawyer can find a jury to agree that DaimlerChrysler knowingly made SUVs that endanger other people on the road. More likely, though, a jury will convict an SUV manufacturer because they believe the Huffington accusation – that SUVs are destroying the Earth, and that they need to be stopped to save the environment, or to reduce dependence on Middle East oil.

Fuel efficiency in North American cars has improved dramatically since the 1970s – the average car is twice as efficient, and light trucks/SUVs are 50% more efficient. But despite that improvement in fuel economy, the U.S. important a far greater share of its oil from the Persian Gulf than it did back in 1973.[73] Even Canada, a great exporter of oil, still imports oil from Arabia, too.[74] So SUVs can't possibly bear the blame for dependence on Middle Eastern oil – nor can they be expected to solve it.

The fact is, better technology, competition from foreign auto makers and consumer demand has helped make today's SUVs more fuel efficient than even small cars from a generation ago. A Dodge Caravan minivan today gets much better gas mileage than a 1978 Volkswagen Beetle, despite that car's iconic image of free love and harmony.

A NEW SUV IS CLEANER THAN AN OLD VW

The improving fuel efficiency means that a new SUV can actually use less gas than a compact car just a few years old.

For example, a five-speed, 2005 Ford Escape SUV[75] is rated at 24 miles per gallon in the city, 29 mpg on the highway. A subcompact automatic 2000 model year Honda Civic[76] rates 28 in the city, 35 on the highway – not much leaner at all. (Bradsher's buddy's Porsche, if it was a 2000 model 911, gets 16 and 25 mpg – making the Ford Escape look, by comparison, almost as clean and lean as an electric car.)

It's not just that today's vehicles, including SUVs, use less gas to begin with – they emit far less pollution. From 1988 to 2004, SUVs and light trucks in North America reduced their average hydrocarbon emissions by more than 90%.[77] And 1988's emission levels were more than 90% less than emissions in 1967.

AN ANTI-SUV ATTACK BACKFIRES

Several years ago, this troublesome fact embarrassed a Toronto anti-SUV activist on live, national TV. The Toronto Environmental Alliance convinced CTV to air a contest: a 1996 Sunfire and a 1996 Jimmy were both brought to an "Emissions Check" in Scarborough. The intro was exciting: "Sport-utility vehicles and minivans are taking over our roads and highways... You might ask yourself: What are they doing to the environment?"[78]

"What Ken and Susan are checking for are the pollutants that cause smog in a city like Toronto. They're looking at hydrocarbons, nitrogen oxides and carbon monoxide... They're testing to see whether the cars are in sync with what they're supposed to be or are they actually gross-polluting, miniature incinerating plants inside this garage?," asked environmentalist Lois Corbett.

The excitement! At last, proof that SUVs are indeed despoilers of nature! And, given that the tester was with the Toronto Environmental Alliance, CTVs viewers would know that they wouldn't be hearing an industry snow-job.

The Sunfire passed the test with flying colours. "The reading on hydrocarbons are about 79," said Corbett. "The limit is 86. So it's actually under." The Sunfire passed the carbon monoxide and nitrogen tests, too.

The tension was incredible. It was like Geraldo Rivera's hit TV show, *The Mystery of Al Capone's Vault* – what would be in that vault? A dead body? Money? Guns? Lois Corbett's *The Mystery of the SUV's Exhaust* was no less tautly produced – and aired on live national TV, too.

At last, anchor Rob Matheson could wait no longer. "Okay, are the results in on the Jimmy yet?" he asked.

"We're just going to go over to the monitor," she said.

It was the moment.

But Corbett sensed something was wrong. There were no sirens, no red lights blinking from the machine. Uh-oh.

"I'm pretty confident that it will pass," she said, trying to soften the coming blow. Moments earlier, she was talking about "gross-polluting, miniature incinerating plants". Now she was looking for excuses. "The real story behind mini-vans isn't going to come up on that screen," she said. Don't believe the machine. Believe her.

Matheson could sense viewers by the hundred reaching for their remote controls, searching for a less painful production. Maybe a Seinfeld re-run was on.

"Okay, we need this quickly, Lois."

"Okay. It's passed with flying colours from a smog emission tailpipe perspective," she finally said. "But from a CO_2 perspective it costs a lot more to run this car."

Say what? Carbon dioxide? But that's not pollution. Carbon dioxide doesn't cause smog. In fact, plants need carbon dioxide to grow. "You'd want to reject this from an environmental perspective because it's pumping way too much CO_2 out into the atmosphere," she said.

But how does she know? The machines at Emissions Check didn't measure CO_2. They measured pollution – that's what

Corbett herself told viewers – and the SUV passed. Corbett wouldn't even tell viewers the SUV's results.

Anyone want to bet it actually beat the little Sunfire?

Like all North American vehicles, SUVs will continue to become safer, cleaner and more fuel-efficient over time. Those might even be reasons why people buy them – or maybe it's for their ability to schlep everything from furniture to groceries to camping equipment. Some of New York's and Hollywood's best media maestros have tried to demonize SUVs, and they've got a lot of attention by doing so. But they haven't slowed down customers' interest in buying the kind of vehicles they like.

But if one keeps in mind the nature of those prosecuting the war on fun – headline hunting politicians like Arianna Huffington, professional activists like David Fenton, and morally superior prudes like Keith Bradsher, the real reasons for the war on SUVs becomes abundantly clear. But as long as smearing SUVs is financially, politically and emotionally profitable for these activists, they'll keep doing it – and maybe one day a haywire jury will do what Bradsher is hoping, and bring down a verdict in an SUV trial – socking an auto manufacturer with a billion-dollar fine, in a mix of environmental hokum, social snobbery and legal adventurism. The battle is definitely not over.

CHAPTER NINETEEN:
THE WAR ON FOOD

Fast foods like Big Macs aren't the only food under assault in the war on fun. They're just the first, because they're the easiest to criticize. But once those "soft targets" are defeated, you can be sure that hundreds of other foods will come under the gun of activists.

Gonzo journalists like Morgan Spurlock are more like clowns than scientists, of course. But there are thousands of health bureaucrats and food scientists promoting *Super Size Me's* anti-food ideology in respectable forums, with the veneer of science that Spurlock could never dream of.

As usual, the anti-food lobbyists use the precedents of the tobacco wars – and, in some cases, even the gun control lobby. Take a recent "study" published[79] by the American Public Health Association, which shows that schools in dense urban environments are typically within a half-mile of a fast food restaurant. It shouldn't take a PhD to come to that conclusion; a half-mile radius in a big city probably puts those kids next to any sort of business you could name – including bars, pool halls and the like. But this study singled out fast food restaurants, and actually compared them to "firearms vendors," concluding that government should "impose stricter controls" on where they are allowed to locate.

Forget for a minute the enormous infringement on economic freedom something like that would entail – the economic freedom of the owners of these restaurants, and that of their existing customers. Look at what's really going on in this study: the moral equivalence being made between firearms and fast food. That's something that Spurlock might say; here, a half-dozen "scientists" conduct a "study" that shows the obvious – fast food restaurants dot the urban landscape, and many of them are near schools. That's not the story here. The story is that a supposedly reputable scientific organization is engaging in subtle demonization of food by comparing those who would sell hamburgers to high schoolers to those who would sell them guns.

CENTER FOR SCIENCE IN THE PUBLIC INTEREST

That kind of overheated rhetoric is the staple of the anti-food groups, who know that taking on the freedom to eat what we like is about as difficult as challenging North Americans' freedom to drive what we like. That's one of the reasons for the analogy with firearms; another is the analogy to illegal drugs. Perhaps the most profligate defamer of food choice is the ironically named Center for Science in the Public Interest, or CSPI.

CSPI was founded as an offshoot of the Center for the Study of Responsive Law, the lobby group founded years ago by perennial far-left U.S. presidential candidate Ralph Nader. Over the past 25 years, the CSPI has grown into a $15-million-a-year lobby group. Some of its larger donors include the professional alarmists at the Nuclear Threat Initiative and the hobby foundation of Hollywood's noisiest complainer, Barbra Streisand.[80]

THE CAFFEINE REVOLT

Like Streisand, the environmental activist who lobbies for energy conservation for others but keeps a massive refrigerated room just for her fur coats, sometimes the folks at CSPI don't quite live up to their rhetoric. When CSPI co-founder Michael Jacobson tried to force his staff to join his anti-caffeine jihad by banning the office coffee machine, he had to back down when a third of his 60 employees threatened to quit over the matter.[81] Jacobson permitted his own staff the freedom to drink coffee – it seems the CSPI staff aren't quite ready to practice what they preach – but that hasn't stopped him from lobbying the governments of Canada and the United States to have your food freedoms circumscribed using the power of the law.

The name Center for Science in the Public Interest is a double-whammy – it implies that the group is based on science, and that it has a public, not private objective. But many of the causes that CSPI fights for can't possibly be called scientific – political is more like it.

Take the CSPI's bias towards vegetarianism. That is a choice for individuals to make; but the CSPI has promoted that personal choice as a scientific and public policy goal. Proper nutrition, says CSPI, "means getting your fats from plants... not animals (meats, milk, cheese and ice cream)."[82] That's one way to get nutrition but it's just one way – both the Canadian[83] and American[84] food guides include meat at a choice; both allow non-meat alternatives for those who so choose. But then the concept of choice isn't really something that the CSPI supports.

CSPI'S ANTI-MEAT AGENDA

Jacobson also serves on the board of the Great American Meatout, an anti-meat event hosted by the Farm Animal Reform Movement (FARM), a radical animal-rights faction that says only vegetarianism is a "nonviolent" diet, and sponsors an annual convention with the slogan "Exposing and challenging the daily terror against animals".[85] This suits the CSPI's major funders just fine, many of whom also donate to FARM, and the anti-meat, anti-fur People for the Ethical Treatment of Animals. FARM and PETA don't call themselves scientists, and don't pretend that they're mainstream enough to go by the name "public interest." That's the CSPI's, job, though they share much of the same radical agenda.

Nowhere does the CSPI's my-way-or-the-highway approach to nutrition sound more jarring than in its campaign against alcohol of any kind. CSPI calls beer "the king of drugs"[86] and opposes the concept of drinking moderately.

"The last thing the world needs is more drinkers, even moderate ones," sermonized the group's newsletter.[87]

Like its other anti-choice campaigns, if the CSPI isn't able to convince individual consumers that they're bad people for drinking in moderation, maybe they can change the law. It's unlikely that the U.S. or Canada would bring back Prohibition, so the next best thing, or so the plan goes, is to demonize anyone associated with alcohol. "Kids in the Crosshairs of Big Booze," screamed the headline of one CSPI news release.[88] Not much science there, not much public interest. But if "Big Booze" is targeting kids – there's that firearms analogy again – then maybe that'll get a new law passed. CSPI has even come out against the National Collegiate Athletic Association (NCAA) and their "Take a Kid to a Game" campaign, designed to get young people interested in sports. CSPI mocks the NCAA's campaign, calling it "Take A Kid to a Beer," and claiming that "Big Beer"[89] is using its advertisements on college sports TV to corrupt North American youth. If sports fans can't be convinced that drinking – even in moderation – is bad, CSPI wants to shame the NCAA into banning beer ads, going to far as to demonize their outreach to urban youth as nothing more than a front for booze. And if that shame campaign won't work on the NCAA, they have other hopes – in the last few pages of their "scientific" study on beer and sports is the text of a proposed law for Congress to pass on the subject.

We know the CSPI staff won their battle against their boss for the right to drink coffee. What we don't know is whether or not their annual Christmas party was allowed to have any eggnog – which contains milk, booze and sugar, a triple no-no over at the CSPI. Then again, maybe Christmas parties themselves are banned at CSPI headquarters.

CHAPTER TWENTY: PERPETUAL WAR

Is there anything that CSPI says is OK to eat? Sounds like a rhetorical question, but Jacobson's answer shows it's not. "CSPI is proud about finding something wrong with practically everything," he told *Washingtonian* magazine.[90] In fact, over the years CSPI has come out against just about every kind of food imaginable. Of course they're against fun foods like chicken wings, and Chinese cuisine. But what on Earth did alfalfa sprouts ever do wrong, or, fat-free cookies, or even home-canned veggies? Do Jacobson's vegetarian allies know about this heresy?

AT LEAST WATER IS OK

CSPIscam.com, a website dedicated to tracking the worst of CSPI's excesses, compiled this staggering list of foods that CSPI has either railed against in its in-house newsletter, or through public campaigns and even lawsuits:[91]

Alfalfa sprouts, Apple pies, Baby food, Bacon, Baked potatoes with sour cream, Baklava, Beef, Beef burritos, Beer, Belgian waffles, Berries, BLT sandwiches, Brie, Buffalo wings, Butter, Caffe latte, Caffe mocha, Caffeine, Candy, Canned fish, Cantaloupes, Cappuccino, Cereals, Cheese, Cheese fries, Cheese manicotti, Cheese nachos, Cheese ravioli, Cheeseburgers, Cheesecake, Chef's salad, Chicken enchiladas, Chicken fingers, Chicken nuggets, Chicken pot pies, Chile rellenos, Chimichangas, Chinese Restaurants, Chocolate cake, Chocolate chips, Chocolate mousse, Clams, Condiments, Cookie dough, Cookies, Corned beef, Crackers, Cream cheese, Cream of broccoli soup, Creamed spinach, Croissants, Danish, Desserts, Dips, Donuts, Eggplant Parmigiana, Eggs, Enchiladas, Family restaurants, Fat-free cakes, Fat-free cookies, Fat-free ice cream, Feta cheese, Food coloring, French fries, French toast, Fried calamari, Fried clams, Fried fish, Fried mozzarella sticks, Fried rice, Fried shrimp, Frozen dinners, Frozen turkey, Fruit cocktails, Fruit drinks, Fruit juice, Fudge brownie sundaes, Garlic bread, General Tso's chicken, Granola bars, Greek salads, Grilled cheese, Gyros, Ham sandwiches, Hamburgers, Home-canned vegetables, Homemade eggnog, Homemade frosting, Hot fudge sundaes, Italian restaurants, Kung pao chicken, Lasagna Lettuce, Lo mein, Luncheon meats, Macaroni and cheese, Margarine, Mayonnaise, Meatloaf, Meat-stuffed grape leaves, Melons, Mexican restaurants, Milk, Milk shakes, Movie popcorn, Mushrooms, Mussels, Olestra, Omelets, Onion rings, Orange beef, Oysters, Pancakes, Pastries, Pizza, Pork chops, Potato chips, Prime rib, Pudding, Quick service restaurants, Rotisserie turkey, Saccharin, Salad dressings, Salads, Salt, Sandwich shops, Sandwiches, Sausage, Scones, Seafood, Seafood restaurants, Shellfish, Soft drinks, Soups, Spaghetti and meatballs, Steakhouses, Stuffed potato skins, Sweet and sour pork, Taco salads, Veal Parmigiana, Waffles and Wine.

Good Lord. Is there anything left besides bread and water? Both butter and margarine are forbidden. Chinese, Mexican and Italian restaurants are no fly zones – sounds rather sweeping. Of course beer and wine are on there; it's surprising that CSPI didn't tell its acolytes to avoid bars altogether.

But here's the trouble with complaining about everything – including salads. If you ring the alarm too often, people will start to ignore it. And when there truly is something dangerous, people will just tune the warning out – like the boy who cried wolf. A whole book has been published of ludicrous warning labels collected on consumer products.[92] Typical is an actual warning label from a hair drier: "Do not use in shower. Never use while sleeping." As the book's author writes, "and never blow-dry your hair while you're sleeping in the shower!"

CRYING WOLF ON FOOD WARNINGS

It's funny, but it's also the don't-cry-wolf principle, and it's the view taken by the U.S. Food and Drug Administration. The FDA is known as heavy-handed and alarmist itself, so when it complains that CSPI-style regulations are too frivolous, it's worth noting.

In 2004, Bill Lockyer, the activist attorney general of the state of California, launched a lawsuit against Tri-Union Seafoods and other tuna canners, claiming that they failed to have conspicuous labels on their products warning about mercury. Lockyer's view of the law as a weapon first made international headlines in 2001 when he commented on another defendant in a California lawsuit. "I would love to personally escort [Enron president Kenneth] Lay to an 8 by 10 cell that he could share with a tattooed dude who says, 'Hi, my name is Spike, honey.'"[93]

That sort of showboating worked well for Lockyer in the Enron suit, and though Chicken of the Sea is hardly the new Enron, Lockyer knew a thing or two about demonizing defendants. Just by filing the suit, he's sounded the alarm, scaring people away from canned fish. But that's exactly the problem, the FDA said in a letter to him.[94] Not only is Lockyer's suit none of this business – food and drug regulations are a federal matter – but Lockyer's suit is not based on sound science.

According to the FDA, their officials require warnings "only in those instances where there is clear evidence of a hazard, in order to avoid overexposing consumers to warnings, which could result in them ignoring all such statements, and hence creating a far greater public health problem." The FDA pointed out that risks of mercury in fish are so remote, and only risky for such a tiny proportion of the population, that a warning might make other people "eat less fish or refrain from eating fish altogether" – which would make for an unhealthy public.

What's worse, says the FDA, Lockyer's lawsuit is based not on science but on a public referendum called Proposition 65 – essentially replacing scientific test with a popular vote. That might make for good politics, but it makes for poor science – and, as the FDA notes, requiring tuna fish producers to publish warnings about their products in the absence of proof would actually be illegal in itself – it would be false advertising. As FDA Commissioner Lester Crawford wrote, "the Proposition 65 warnings purport to convey factual information, namely that methylmercury is known to cause cancer and reproductive harm. However, it is done without any scientific basis as to the possible harm caused by the particular foods in question, or as to the amounts of such foods that would be required to cause this harm."

"Stated differently, these warnings omit facts which are necessary to place the information in its proper context. As a result, FDA believes that the Proposition 65 warnings are misleading... causing tuna products with such warnings to be misbranded under federal law. Tuna manufacturers would not be able to comply both with Proposition 65 and the Act." In other words, Lockyer was trying to get them to break the law.

Now, the FDA itself is a notorious risk-monger when it comes to food; but at least, unlike Lockyer, they actually conduct scientific studies first. "The FDA has been studying the issue of methylmercury in fish for several years," the regulator reports. "As a result, the agency believes that it is uniquely qualified to determine how to handle the public health concerns related to methylmercury in fish." Translation: Lockyer doesn't have the foggiest idea of what he's talking about.

CHAPTER TWENTY-ONE:
BUREAUCRATS INSTEAD OF WILLPOWER

One of CSPI's mottos is "Because it takes more than willpower." That's their way of saying if they can't convince you to do the right thing – if you don't agree with them that meat is bad, for example, or if you think they might be right but realize there's more to life than being afraid of living – then CSPI wants someone else to make your choices for you. It's infantilization, turning every grown adult into a child who needs to be looked after, even against his or her wishes. It's not just an insult to the freedom of every adult – and of parents to decide for their children – but it's an intellectual insult, too. It's CSPI's way of saying that they can never be wrong, that they don't need to convince you, because even if they can't, they'll find some way to make you obey them – like Bill Lockyer's illegal lawsuits, throwing the power of the state at anyone who happens to like tuna sandwiches.

TAKING ON AUNT JEMIMA

Sometimes, CSPI can be more comical than serious, such as their threatened lawsuit against Aunt Jemima, to change the label on blueberry waffles from "artificially flavored blueberry bits" to CSPI's preferred wording, "with imitation blueberries." Pinnacle Foods, which owns the Aunt Jemima brand, agreed to the change to avoid the nuisance lawsuit. CSPI was so proud of this momentous public health moment that it put out a gloating press release[95], and confirmed that "no actual blueberries are harmed in making Aunt Jemima Blueberry Waffles." That's probably a joke, but with CSPI's radical vegetarian philosophy, it wouldn't be surprising if one day they started suing companies for harming fruits. (Perhaps CSPI should congratulate Pinnacle for not using real berries, which are on CSPI's don't-eat list, above.)

No doubt Michael Jacobson and, well, at least two-thirds of the staff at CSPI really want everyone to live and eat like them. But it's not individual consumers and eaters of food who should be the most worried. CSPI's lawsuits, and those of other activist lawyers of fortune, and even attorneys general like Bill Lockyer, won't target individuals – they'll go after the deepest pockets around. That's why groups like CSPI are already laying down the kind of junk science and junk legal arguments to lay the groundwork for lawsuits against companies, ranging from the NCAA to McDonald's to "Big Beer."

ATTACKING PARENTAL RESPONSIBILITY

In 2003, CSPI rolled out another "study," financed in part by the Park Foundation (which also gives grants to animal rights groups). The purpose was obvious: to lay the groundwork for a tobacco-style lawsuit by painting restaurants and food companies as devious schemers who deliberately try to turn children against their parents, in order to sell them unhealthy food. The study itself was called "Pestering Parents."[96] It was a frontal attack on the common sense reply that parents are responsible for what their children eat. By blaming "big business," as the report does, and excusing parents, the "study" lays the groundwork for lawsuits by preempting the obvious defence that household eating is determined by parents. Pestering Parents also calls any minor a "child" and calls for an outright ban on any advertising to such "children" – children who are old enough to drive, vote and join the army.

The recommendations in Pestering Parents don't just talk about health; they talk about a government strategy that reaches deep into schools, grocery stores, the media and even families to re-engineer how we eat. If it sounds invasive, it is – remember, to CSPI, willpower is not enough. Pestering Parents calls for the government to pester just about anyone – even directing doctors to pester families about "television viewing/marketing and their effects." Is that really what a trip to the pediatrician is about – political propaganda? But your doctor would just be the beginning; the CSPI wants to "implement media literacy programs to teach children the purpose of advertising and how to identify and resist advertising and other marketing techniques." Presumably, CSPI's propaganda that pediatricians would now be forced to recite would not be deemed an advertisement worthy of "resistance."

THE CANADIAN EXPERIENCE

In 2004, Canada's leading children's advertisers did just what you'd think the folks at CSPI would want – they started an ad campaign focused on emphasizing healthier lifestyle choices and even so-called media literacy. The Concerned Children's Advertisers, the group that started the initiative, is made up of nearly every TV station in the country, toymakers, food companies and ad agencies – with representatives from Canada's federal departments of health and justice, as well as the Canadian Radio-Television and Telecommunications Commission, or CRTC, the regulator for TV and radio in the country.

The Concerned Children's Advertisers produced a series of a dozen different ads, ranging from healthy eating, to exercise, to resisting peer pressure, to anti-bullying messages to even messages encouraging kids to be skeptical of TV ads – it was as if the Pestering Parents to-do list had been voluntarily done by children's advertisers (except, of course, for ordering doctors to give TV watching advice).

The response from CSPI? Outrage, of course – how dare candy makers, snack makers, soft drink makers and cereal makers steal the CSPI's thunder! They were supposed to play their pre-assigned role: the evil "big businesses" that CSPI alone would take on. How else was CSPI supposed to raise its money, if it didn't have any bogeymen to rail against?

CAN'T TAKE YES FOR AN ANSWER

The CSPI's Canadian branch plant churned out an angry press release, sputtering that the "so-called Concerned Children's Advertisers" didn't "truly" care about Canadian kids as much as the U.S.-based CSPI. It was a "cynical exercise in public relations" and that no food company could possibly be committed to the well being of kids. "The profound conflict of interest, hypocrisy and audacity of mounting this campaign could make even tobacco executives' eyes pop," wailed the CSPI's man in Canada, Bill Jeffery, in a press release.[97]

Jeffery's attack didn't spend much time criticizing the Concerned Children's Advertisers ads themselves – other than slamming an ad that suggested more exercise could offset the eating of snack food. Rather, it focused on calling into question the motives and good faith of anyone who sells products – or even broadcasts TV shows – to kids. That was the part of the CSPI's response that had the highest voltage: they couldn't believe that advertisers were honing in on their turf of being righteous. Hey, being noble and public-minded was the CSPI's job – it was even in their name! What would that do to CSPI's moral preening if the big bad companies weren't being big and bad?

There is no way for the food industry to appease people like the CSPI because, by definition, they would cease to exist if people actually did what they demanded. That's why the CSPI has to react to violently even to – no, especially to – positive steps, like the one taken voluntarily by Canada's children's advertisers. It's the reason why Jacobson says he's proud of finding a problem with just about any food out there; it's the reason his no-eat list now includes alfalfa sprouts and berries. The moment the CSPI has nothing left to fight will be the moment the foundation money dries up. They are truly a perpetual motion machine – and, until the lawyers-of-fortune use the CSPI's drumbeat against food manufacturers to score a tobacco-style, super-sized lawsuit against "big food," it's certain that they'll keep going, too.

KILLED BY A SALT-SHAKER

It's not just the CSPI, of course, though they are the central clearing house for the war on food, and they claim 900,000 readers of their monthly "nutrition" magazine across North America. There are plenty of others out there attacking the foods we love. But the CSPI imbues loony notions with a scientific imprimatur that other groups just couldn't get away with. Take the opening line of their 2005 report on regular table salt: "Salt – sodium chloride – is perhaps the deadliest ingredient in the food supply."[98] That sounds exciting – and calling salt by its chemical name makes it sound even deadlier, just like dihydrogen oxide sounds riskier than tap water. But studies by less partisan scientists[99] show that reducing salt – even reducing salt dramatically – doesn't have a provable effect on the death rate and that "no single universal prescription for sodium intake can be scientifically justified."[100]

CHAPTER TWENTY-TWO:
WHEN CONVENTIONAL WISDOM IS WRONG

One of the practical tests for fanaticism is to ask someone what facts it would take to change their mind. That is, could they ever be convinced that their beliefs were wrong? Is there anything that would cause them to discard their particular theory of the world – or, if the facts were inconvenient, would they ignore the facts and just hold on to the theory? Or has their political view become a religion to them, unshakable and based on faith or maybe, as in the case of so many in the war on fun, based on a feeling of moral superiority?

So much of the war on fun is based on a certain theory of life in desperate search of facts – and that has led to a whole industry of junk science, where pseudo-studies are manufactured to buttress ideological arguments. Trouble is, most journalists aren't equipped – or worse, choose not – to tell the difference between junk science and real science.

THE MYTH OF MAN-MADE GLOBAL WARMING

Take the argument that SUVs cause global warming – an argument repeated so many times it is taken as conventional wisdom, when in fact there is simply no science to support it. It is true that the Earth is very gently and very slowly warming as the world recedes from a little ice age 150 years ago[101]; but that warming trend started far before the automobile was invented. Anyone who has heard of the great ice ages in the Earth's past, and knows we're not in one now, could deduce that the world's climate has gone through natural cycles before, and will continue to do so. In fact, it was just a generation ago when fashionable scientists warned that Earth was threatened by global cooling.[102] "The Cooling World," *Newsweek*, April 28, 1975.

But ever since the 1992 Rio convention on climate change, the theory of man-made global warming has been repeated so often that it is accepted as fact, and de-industrialization, as contemplated in the Kyoto Protocol of 1997, is considered a real solution. But even the Kyoto Protocol's authors and staunchest defenders – the high priests of the religion of global warming – acknowledge that even if every country in the world were to meet its Kyoto cutbacks of energy use, global warming would not be stopped at all. According to the U.N.'s Intergovernmental Panel on Climate Change, if every country cut its greenhouse gas emissions sharply enough to comply with the Kyoto Protocol, the total effect on the world's climate would be just 0.2 degrees Celsius by the year 2100.[103] And that's what the treaty's believers say!

GREENHOUSE EFFECT IS NATURAL

The fact is, the so-called greenhouse effect has been around a lot longer than industrialization – and it's a good thing, too. The greenhouse effect, where the atmosphere traps the sun's heat, like a greenhouse, is what keeps the Earth warm, as opposed to, say, the kind of atmosphere on the moon, which has no greenhouse gases. Without greenhouse gases, there would be no life on Earth.

Of course, these gases were around long before SUVs were; the most ubiquitous greenhouse gas is water vapour. Naturally occurring carbon dioxide and methane are the next two most common greenhouse gases, and they're the ones regulated by Kyoto. But the amount of greenhouse gas emitted by every vehicle in North America, compared to naturally occurring greenhouse gases, is so small as to be imperceptible. You could take every vehicle off the road – not just SUVs, but all motorcycles, cars and heavy-duty trucks, too, and you wouldn't even make a 1% dent in the total annual emissions of greenhouse gases.[104]

1 VOLCANO = 7 YEARS OF INDUSTRY

Thinking that mankind has caused the Earth to warm is height of arrogance. It's not the belief of an environmentally sensitive person, but rather the belief of an environmentally illiterate person, who believes that the world's climate literally begins and ends with him. In fact, a single, week-long eruption of Mt. Pinatubo's volcano in 1991 spewed out more greenhouse gases than seven years worth of all of Canada's factories and cars combined.[105]

NO SCIENTIFIC CONSENSUS

Banning SUVs isn't about stopping global warming. Global warming is the after-the-fact excuse for banning SUVs, once all of the anti-terrorism or road safety arguments have been debunked. More than 17,000 of the world's leading climatologists and scientists from other, related disciplines, have challenged the science behind the Kyoto Protocol, including a number of the scientists on the UN panel whose work was used to draft the treaty.[106] But to try to defend SUVs by relying on science is to miss the point here: SUV-haters don't want to be on the side of science, they want science to be on their side. If it's not, they're not going to change their minds – they're just going to change their arguments.

HARMLESS CELL PHONES

Cell phones are another area where critics – in this case, mass-tort litigators such as Peter Angelos – are impervious to science. Every major study has failed to show a link between cell phone use and cancer, including a massive Danish study that compared 420,000 cell phone users in that country to the national cancer registry. The results: "No excesses were observed for cancers of the brain or nervous system." A similar study involving 285,000 U.S. cell phone users found only one area where cell phones were deadly: "

107

motor vehicle collisions."[107] That's too bad, but it's hardly the cancer scare that Angelos was lusting after. It hasn't stopped him from suing, of course.

Food critics have been some of the worst purveyors of junk science – and ignorers of real science. But the so-called child obesity epidemic used to whip up public interest just doesn't exist. A recent survey from the U.K. Department of Health shows that the average weight of girls 3 to 15 years of age increased just one pound from 1995 to 2003, and for boys the number actually fell slightly during the same period.[108] There's no obesity epidemic amongst kids – there's just a bored press corps too ready to retype the anti-food lobbyists' press releases without criticism.

THE FRAMINGHAM STUDY

One of the most authoritative studies of cardiovascular disease is the Framingham study, named after a small town in Massachusetts where more than 5,000 men and women agreed to have their heart health studied for their whole lives – and now a second generation of Framinghamites has signed up, too. According to that study, the thinnest men had the shortest life expectancy, whereas men 25% to 40% above the government's "ideal" weight lived the longest. For women, death rates were higher than normal only for the very thin and very fat.[109]

The Framingham study is not a license to overeat; but it is an authoritative, non-partisan reality check to the Chicken Littles of the anti-food lobby who have declared obesity a national calamity and have gone to war against anything with an ounce of fat or a shake of salt in it. The entire focus of the anti-food lobby is to blame food companies, or the food itself, for people's health – thus the demonization of food company executives as scheming tricksters, trying to take advantage of helpless kids. But in fact science suggests it's not what kids eat that makes them fat or not – it's how active they are.

According to a study at Queen's University in Kingston, Ontario, a study of 137,000 kids in 34 countries shows that, surprisingly, "the frequency of sweets intake was lower in overweight than normal weight youth." The fat kids actually ate less candy and drank less pop – they just didn't exercise as much.[110] The Queen's study confirms a 2004 Harvard study following American kids over a three-year period. According to the study, snack foods, including sugary soft drinks, did "not meaningfully change the results . . . there was not a strong association between intake of snack foods and weight gain." And a 2004 University of California study showed the same thing: "Of the 7 dietary and physical activity variables examined in this cross-sectional study, insufficient vigorous physical activity was the only risk factor for higher body mass index for adolescent boys and girls." Snacks or not, fruits and veggies or not, the only thing that made kids fat, according to these studies, was whether or not they exercised. That's not something that can be pinned on Ronald McDonald.

CHAPTER TWENTY-THREE:
THE URBAN LEGEND OF SECOND-HAND SMOKE

If some of these studies sound counterintuitive to us, it's because SUVs, cell phones and fast food are demonized, defamed a little bit more every day. Endless repetition in the media about their harm starts to build up a conventional wisdom, so when an lobbyist repeats the charge, even without some sort of junk science back-up, the charge has a ring of credibility to it – the SUV/global warming connection is a powerful example.

But no industry has been so utterly undone by junk science as has smoking. What was once a commonplace, almost patriotic habit, is now so reviled in the conventional wisdom that any charge, no matter how half-baked, sticks to the industry. That's no accident; decades of demonization have turned public opinion against tobacco companies – and that's borne great fruit for anti-tobacco lawyers when it comes to jury selection for the big trials.

Let us grant that smoking is not a healthy habit. But how about second-hand smoke? That is the new frontier for the war on smoking, because it provides the moral cover for stopping even voluntary, adult smokers from lighting up, by implying that they are forcing others to endure their health risks. It's the rationale to ban all indoor smoking, to forbid restaurants from having smoking sections, and it's just the right thing to prop up the moral superiority of the anti-smoking activists – smokers don't just hurt themselves, they hurt others, including their own children!

SMOKE ON TRIAL

But while second-hand smoke might be annoying to some, the fact is it has never been proved to be a health risk, period. In fact, the Environmental Protection Agency report on

110

second-hand smoke that launched the thousands of attacks on tobacco was nullified in a 1998 U.S. federal court hearing, by a judge who called the study a political fraud.[111]

Judge William Osteen who heard the case was no sure bet for the tobacco industry; he had been the judge who ruled that nicotine was a drug and that the FDA should regulate it. But in the case of the EPA's second-hand smoke study, Judge Osteen found that the EPA had decided to oppose second-hand smoke as a policy before it even conducted the scientific tests to prove that outcome. They hid their scientific results when they weren't politically correct, they ignored data that didn't conform to the preconceptions and they generally substituted politics for science. In fact, the only way the EPA could find that second-hand smoke was risky was by throwing out their standard scientific methodology, and finding another one that gave them the answer they were looking for.[112] According to the judge, the "EPA publicly committed to a conclusion before research had begun."[113]

POLITICS AHEAD OF SCIENCE

According to Judge Osteen's thorough review of the EPA study, that agency had violated the government's research procedures, suppressed findings that were contrary to its political goals, ignored the EPA's own Risk Criteria Office, excluded studies that contradicted their preconceptions and, after all that, couldn't find a statistically significant correlation between second-hand smoke and health risks. It was a stunning setback to the "science" of the anti-smoking lobby. But by 1998 when the Osteen decision was handed down, the anti's had been dining out on the second-hand smoke campaign for five years. With or without the EPA study behind them, the "fact" of second-hand smoke's risk was already established in the public's mind.

The EPA appealed the Osteen decision, but not on the science – they claimed that Judge Osteen didn't have jurisdiction to review their study, and the U.S. Court of Appeals for the Fourth Circuit granted that appeal in 2002, but without vindicating the EPA's science.

AMERICAN CANCER SOCIETY STUDY

Studies about second-hand smoke continue, as other more ethical epidemiologists genuinely try to measure the health risks. One massive study, published in the *British Medical Journal* in 2003, tracked 118,000 people who enrolled in an American Cancer Society test in 1959, and followed them until 1998. The study focused on the 35,000 people who never smoked but who lived with smokers – that's 40 years of breathing in second hand smoke.

The results? "No significant associations were found for current or former exposure to environmental tobacco smoke" (the medical phrase for second-hand smoke). "The results do not support a causal relation between environmental tobacco smoke and tobacco related mortality, although they do not rule out a small effect. The association between exposure to environmental tobacco smoke and coronary heart disease and lung cancer may be considerably weaker than generally believed."[114]

The study referred to the earlier EPA study and others, pointing out a likely flaw: "Exposure to environmental tobacco smoke is difficult to measure quantitatively and therefore has been approximated by self reported estimates, primarily smoking history in spouses," said the researchers. "Confounding by active cigarette smoking is so strong that the association with environmental tobacco smoke can only be evaluated among never smokers." In other words, the only way to make sure that a study is truly measuring the effects of second-hand smoke and not direct smoking is to isolate people who never smoke – and that's what the massive study did.

THE BLACK DOG PUB

Despite the continuing science showing no statistically valid relationship between second-hand smoke and health, the fib has taken root; no politician would dare to fight the conventional wisdom on that one. It's tough to fight against a fib like second-hand smoke. But some bar owners are trying. The Black Dog Pub, a popular restaurant and bar in Toronto's Scarborough region invested in a ventilation system similar to the ones used in Las Vegas casinos to keep the air fresh and smoke-free.

Anti-smoking activists like to joke that a non-smoking section of a restaurant is like a non-peeing section of a pool. It's funny because it's true. But the metaphor doesn't hold up if the two swimmers aren't in a pool, but in a stream, and the "offender" is downstream from the other swimmer. That's what the Black Dog's ventilation system does: it creates a slow and steady breeze of fresh air from the non-smoking section to the smoking section, and then out the building. Non-smokers never get any second-hand smoke, and smokers themselves quickly have their own smoke whisked away from them.

The Black Dog became a bit of a political sensation in Toronto when it first installed its ventilation system, because Toronto was embarking on an anti-smoking crackdown, and hotel and restaurant owners saw the system as a way of solving the health bureaucrats' concerns without gutting their business. So the Black Dog's air quality was tested by the Center for Toxicology and Environmental Health in Little Rock, Arkansas.[115] They found that the air in the non-smoking section of the restaurant had an 80% reduction in "respirable particulates" – that is, smoke – and up to 90% reduction in other tobacco components. Interestingly, the smoking section of the restaurant itself was 70% less smoky, too – right in the middle of the smoking section itself.

CLEANER THAN A NO-SMOKING BAR

Of course, the ventilation didn't just clean up the cigarette smoke, but all sorts of other airborne particles too, everything from regular dust to kitchen grease. According to the Little Rock lab, the Black Dog's air was as clean as an average mall food court that was completely smoke free.

The Black Dog's customers loved it, of course. Since installing the ventilation, they won the "Best Pub" award three times, as well as the "Business of the Year Award" by the local Chamber of Commerce.[116] But such happiness would only make smoke come out of the ears of the anti-smoking activists. The Ontario Campaign for Action on Tobacco, one of dozens of government-supported anti-smoking lobby groups, saw the Black Dog for what it was: a practical solution that could stop the second-hand smoke argument in its tracks, by simply eliminating it.

OCAT launched an entire Internet campaign to smear the ventilation plan, publishing private investigator-style background files on anyone involved with the project (though they didn't mention the "Best Pub" award). Though the Black Dog's customers love going there, OCAT did manage to persuade the regulators at Health Canada not to test the air themselves. They gleefully published a memo[117] from an assistant deputy minister of health explaining why.

NO COMPROMISE ALLOWED

"The problem with ventilation as an exposure reduction strategy," wrote Ian Potter, "is that exposure, even if the system is operating at maximum efficiency, is never zero. In other words, in the best-case scenario, there is an explicit acceptance of some level of exposure to non-smokers." So now not even a single particle of smoke is permissible; the anti-smoking lobbyists and their cousins in the government bureaucracy would rather have an all or nothing smoking situation, rather than a 90% reduction. This isn't about regulation of smoke, or reasonable management of health risks; it's about prohibition.

"Since no ventilation system will protect everybody," continued Potter, "and might even delude non-smokers into a false sense of protection, it is concluded that such systems are not as good as a total ban." The second-hand smoke study of the EPA was proved false; the American Cancer Society's study showing no harm remains the state of the art. The Black Dog's toxicology lab shows that it is just as clean as any non-smoking restaurant in town. But the anti's refuse to test it – refuse even to examine it! – for fear that their relentless drive towards prohibition will come apart in the face of a new technology that allows smokers and non-smokers to co-exist.

Of course Potter refuses to study ventilation; of course OCAT's response is not to learn about ventilation, but to demonize its proponents. Because if there is a scientific solution to second-hand smoke, they'll lose their chief weapon in their battle against personal freedom – they'll lose the ability to demonize smokers as callous inflicters of disease on their neighbors. God help us.

CHAPTER TWENTY-FOUR:
WHY POLITICIANS LISTEN TO THE ANTI'S

If the kind of zealotry that animates the anti's were limited to the anti's themselves, the world would be a safer – or at least friendlier – place than it is. Smokers would smoke; non-smokers wouldn't. Everyone would make their own eating choices – and parents, not governments, would look after their own kids. Snobs would still be snobs, and Arianna Huffington would still look down on SUV owners, but no one would be able to force anyone else to do anything. It's called freedom.

Except that it doesn't quite work that way in practice. In politics, the squeaky wheel gets the grease, and groups like the Center for Science in the Public Interest are masters at getting media coverage. At least that lobby group derives its income from its newsletter readers and from private foundations – across North America, most anti-smoking organizations are either appendages of public health agencies, or, as in Canada, receive direct funding from the government... to lobby those same governments. The government itself actually encourages the wheel to squeak.

And while severely normal citizens are going about their business, these self-appointed busybodies are lobbying up a storm, pressing their agenda, twisting arms of politicians, and schmoozing the media with great success. Simply the chronic repetition of their ideas – especially their demonization and marginalization of any one they disagree with, from "Big Beer" to "Detroit" – has an effect.

Ideas that are once on the fringe, if repeated enough, become conventional wisdom in legislatures. The threat of global warming – once a doomsday scenario only invoked by Greenpeace fundraisers – is now accepted as scientific fact. And though the so-called scientific consensus has unraveled on man-made global warming, the train has already left the station on Canada's Kyoto implementation plan – the taxes are being imposed, and the imaginary hot air credits are being readied for sale.[118]

"That's the exact same calculation that politicians make when they hike taxes on cigarettes and alcohol, too. They know that tobacco and alcohol executives don't dare speak out in public; even the name of the taxes – "sin taxes" – compounds the conventional wisdom that these are bad people making bad products, and they should just consider themselves lucky that we don't have Prohibition anymore. Individual smokers and drinkers aren't likely to kick up a fuss about an extra dollar on a pack of cigarettes. And smokers and drinkers don't naturally group together for political action – it's not a natural grassroots interest group, unlike, say, members of the same religion or industry. Big, wealthy anti-smoking lobbies can hire full-time activists to raise a ruckus in the press and keep the pressure on in the lobbies of power. Ordinary smokers and drinkers aren't even there. Who's going to win that battle?

POLITICIANS LOVE THE PRESS COVERAGE

But it's not just that the anti's are well armed and focused while foodies are too busy having fun at restaurants to care. It's that the reality for most politicians in Canada and the U.S. is anonymity – and cockamamie campaigns are a ticket to media coverage, the elixir of modern politics. Only a chosen few Members of Parliament get appointed to cabinet, and most of those are never heard from again. Only a handful of MPs can stand up in Question Period each day, and even that's only in those months when Parliament is sitting.

In the U.S., the challenge is different. The political landscape is dotted with dominant congressmen and senators, many of whom have been in office for decades. Try being a junior congressman from Arizona, competing every day for press coverage with that human microphone, Senator John

McCain.

So ambitious politicians from both countries face the same challenge: how do they make a splash – but a good splash, the kind that makes them look like they're fighting for the little guy? Championing an obscure bill, even one with no chance of passage, is a sure ticket to TV coverage. Where's the downside? Lots of media attention, building a reputation as someone who stands up to Big Tobacco/Beer/Sugar/SUV, and getting plenty of campaign donations from the anti's to boot. More than one political career has been made that way.

That's surely the story of Tom Wappel, the otherwise forgettable Canadian MP from Scarborough Southwest. Since 1993, Wappel has struggled to make a name for himself by championing the idea that every restaurant in Canada and every grocery store public conspicuous nutritional guides to every single food item they sell right on their menu. As Wappel told Parliament, "even if the smallest full-service restaurant chain . . . had to do a full chemical analysis for every menu item at $350 each . . . the total would involve a maximum one time cost of $35,000."[119] Well, that's certainly a relief – how many waitresses or busboys will lose their jobs over this foisted cost onto restaurants, a cost to be replicated every time a menu is changed or a new food item introduced?

Wappel's bill would require menus to have detailed info on fat, calories and other information printed right next to every menu item – and even for menu add-ons or different combinations. As one MP pointed out, a submarine shop with 15 different toppings has more than 40,000 possible combinations – how is that supposed to comply?[120]

Wappel's bill still hasn't become law, but it has got his name in the media – and forged an alliance with the Center for Science in the Public Interest, who Wappel thanked as he introduced the proposal. Wappel named Bill Jeffery, CSPI's

Canadian agent, "for his hard work in helping me to prepare the bill and some of the arguments that I have put forward... I would also like to thank the Center for Science in the Public Interest."[121] The CSPI isn't just a group of radical animal rights activists in the U.S. They're the drafter of proposed draconian food regulations in Canada, too.

Nutters like Tom Wappel often don't get far with their bills – in a democratic Parliament or Congress, there are usually enough politicians asking the tough questions on behalf of restaurants and their employees – and customers. But in less democratic bodies, like the United Nations, the CSPIs of the world go unchecked.

ANTI'S AT THE U.N.

Take the World Health Organization, the health arm of the United Nations. Like so many other tentacles of the UN, it has outgrown its original mandate of disease eradication and has moved into micro-managing the health of the UN's member states – without a democratic mandate.

Normally, what a bunch of foreign diplomats gathered at exotic locales have to say about what people in Toronto or Chicago eat is irrelevant. But the purpose of the WHO and the hundreds of Non-Governmental Organizations, or NGOs, who lobby it is to build up a body of "science" or "law" that is then imported into member countries like Canada and the U.S.

CSPI Canada's Bill Jeffery, for example, told a recent WHO meeting in Geneva[122] that the world's anti-food lobbyists should use UNICEF – the "Children's Emergency Fund" – to pressure governments in North America to ban advertising to children, as if that was on par with its mandate to eliminate deaths from malaria in the Third World. That report included a lengthy legal opinion with such gems as "there is a sound basis for interpreting the 'right to health' as embracing a right to be free from commercial influences that *may* erode health"[123] and that the "International Covenant of Civil and Political Rights... calls for governments to ensure that their citizens receive balanced information about the health risks of consuming certain foods."[124]

It's not just food – that's just the latest battlefield. The international lobbying effort against tobacco is well developed, and having maxed out in North America, is headed for the third world, especially China. The Kyoto Protocol is a dead letter as a treaty, with the United States Senate having voted unanimously to forbid its implementation if to do so would harm the U.S. economy relative to Europe's. Despite that, the junk science behind Kyoto is now received wisdom, with no debate permitted – and is now the law in countries like Japan and, soon, Canada.

The world-wide battle against SUVs hasn't taken root in legislation, yet, other than constant attempts by anti's to regulate SUVs out of existence using fuel economy laws. But to the lawyers, lobbyists and junk scientists driving the anti movement, that's just what you call a green pasture.

CHAPTER TWENTY-FIVE:
HOW TO FIGHT BACK

What can be done to stop the war on fun? It's a problem that's been decades in the making, and it won't be solved overnight. It's a problem of ideas, mainly, and it has to be fought that way – merely stopping a lawsuit here or a bad piece of legislation there isn't enough. The popular culture has to be cured of this statist Prohibitionism.

Most of the fighting will have to be done by the industries targeted by the anti's; there really isn't a lot that ordinary consumers can do to fight lawsuits or regulations, other than to continue to proudly exercise their own freedom to choose what they buy at restaurants, grocery stores, auto dealer- ships and tobacconists. But that is an important step in itself: to fight, on a day-by-day basis, the shunning that the anti's have fomented, the social pariah status of those who choose to smoke or drive SUVs. A common theme in all of the bat- tles in the war on fun is the demonization of what was once considered a normal, even respectable lifestyle. On winter days, smokers huddle outside doorways of public building, catching a few puffs before scurrying back inside from the cold. They are the very manifestation of people who have been marginalized. How long before fast food restaurants are delegitimized, and become as disreputable as, say, adult video stores? The answer lies as much with what political fashions individual people accepts, as with laws passed by the state.

INDUSTRY MUST FIGHT BACK

But the real battle against the war on fun won't come from grassroots people – it must come from the captains of the industries that are under attack. It might be too late for the cigarette industry, and it's almost high noon for the food

industry, though that battle is not yet lost. The SUV manufacturers have a little more time than that. But if you trace
the cycle of the war on tobacco, you can see precisely where
the war on food and the war on SUVs are – perhaps ten and
fifteen years behind the curve respectively.

WHAT WOULD TOBACCO DO?

What would tobacco manufacturers do differently if they
could turn back the clock twenty years, if they could deal
with a general public that had not yet been taught to despise
them and that had not heard the false, junk science statistics
repeated so often that they have become conventional
wisdom? Would they have taken a different approach?
Undoubtedly they would have – and it would have started
with an error that the tobacco executives made that is
standard operating procedure for anyone faced with a
stunning crisis: denial of the threats it faced.

How could tobacco, the crop that built the New World –
the industry that counted amongst its "executives" many of
America's Founding Fathers – ever fall from grace? It was
unthinkable – and so the opening salvos of the anti-cigarette
lobby were brushed off, or, at best, answered only in the
courts of law. But in the court of public opinion, seeds were
being planted that, over time, would grow enough to make
tobacco a demonized product, label its users tasteless, and
deem its producers criminals.

FIVE STRATEGIES FOR FIGHTING BACK

There are five key strategies to fighting back in the war on
food and the war on SUVs. Had the tobacco companies used
them, their fate may have been different – smoking would be
regarded for what it is, a personal choice, and an entire generation of lawyers of fortune might have been directed into
more productive work.

1. CHOOSING THE LANGUAGE OF THE BATTLE

The language of the war on cigarettes is so ingrained in popular culture we don't even notice it anymore – even smoking advocates use it. Take the simple phrase "second-hand smoke." It even sounds dirty, like re-breathing someone's air. Imagine getting into a tub of "second-hand bath water." It wasn't always called that; researchers call it sidestream smoke, or environmental tobacco smoke. But those words didn't carry the negative connotation. So the anti's kept repeating their preferred, slightly pejorative phrase over and over again with great discipline until it became the standard terminology.

Or take a more obvious slur: labeling anyone in the smoking industry part of "big tobacco." There are indeed big tobacco companies, but there are small ones, too. And when retailers of cigarettes are included, it's fair to say that the average unit of the smoking industry is the mom and pop corner store – hardly big anything. But if cigarette companies can be dehumanized, and given an insulting name – a big, alien, distant name – it makes it a lot easier to denounce.

These tactics can be seen in the battles against food and SUVs, too. CSPI regularly used the epithet "big food" – and not to describe large servings of food, but rather the murky executives that dreamt up the Double Big Mac. "Big beer" is another favorite of theirs, and again it refers to brewing companies, not a large pitcher. The food police have been especially creative, convincing even the judge who heard an anti-McDonald's lawsuit to describe Chicken McNuggets as "Frankenfoods." Catchy – and that's the point. When you own the language, the debate is half won already.

Most of the food and auto industry still doesn't believe that they're under a tobacco-style assault. They just can't imagine the day will come when they will marginalized the dame way. But one fight-back group, the Center for Consumer Freedom, has seen the importance of language in the coming battle. Even their name shows they know this war will be won or lost in the court of public opinion before it gets to the court of law. By choosing the name "Consumer Freedom," the group has built in two effective messages: they're about consumers – ordinary families, not "big," bad companies – and they're about personal freedom, that building block of our society, that thing we've gone to war to protect. Of course, the Consumer Freedom people will still be labeled as agents of "Big Food," but the mere speaking of their name makes a point. The Center for Science in the Public Interest packed three loaded terms into their name, the Consumer Freedom people will make do with two.

Another smart counter-punch in the war on fun comes from the SUV Owners of America. Its name, too, shifts the battle away from "Big Auto," as Arianna Huffington's "Detroit Project" would call it, and moves it to countless individual soccer moms and car pool families across the country. It's about owners, all across America – not big executives holed up in Detroit.

Both the Center for Consumer Freedom and the SUVOA emphasize another popular value: choice. It's a desirable value amongst consumers – to have a choice is the very essence of North American shopping, eating and driving. But it also carries political overtones from the 1960s, tapping into a vein of personal libertarianism, perhaps even appealing to left-leaning observers who might normally tend towards government intervention. "Keep your laws off my body" is a feminist slogan referring to reproductive organs, but it also works as a slogan about what one does with a stomach, too. Former Canadian Liberal Prime Minister Pierre Trudeau once said the "state had no place in the bedrooms of the nation." If that's the case, should it have a place in the kitchens of the nation? There are liberal, or at least libertarian arguments against the war on fun, and by using words like "choice" and "freedom," advocates that might naturally garner support from conservatives would appeal to many liberals' sense of privacy, too.

2. FIGHTING JUNK SCIENCE

Inflammatory or appealing language only goes so far, of course; there has to be substance behind it. And that is another of the great mistakes that the cigarette industry made: It let urban legends and popular myths about cigarettes harden into "truths" that "everybody knows." Second-hand smoke is the best example of this – a near-universally accepted fact that just isn't true. And though rigorously scientific research, and even a large trial of the EPA's own investigations into the matter, show that second-hand smoke has never been proved harmful, conventional wisdom is so resolved on the point that to dispute it today would be akin to claiming that the Earth is flat.

It's easy to understand how such a myth could be built – it has a certain plausibility to it, and was repeated endlessly before any rebuttals were put forward. But that exact same strategy is happening now in food. And the latest victims of these smears are making the same mistakes again.

Morgan Spurlock's *Super Size Me* was packed full of spin, junk science, inconsistencies and plain old lies. But the movie was entertaining and visual – just like his old gross-out show where he dared people to eat jars of mustard or bricks of butter. The film only grossed $11-million in the U.S., and never opened in more than 230 theaters nation-wide.[125] But the secondary news coverage of the movie – most of it fawning – helped solidify Spurlock's gonzo accusations into "facts" about McDonald's. It didn't help things that the movie repeatedly showed Spurlock calling McDonald's public relations department and leaving message after message – the image was that of a "big" company trying to stonewall "the little guy." McDonald's see no evil, speak no evil approach continued after the movie was released, too, saying as little as it could, just hoping that noisy man and his camera crews would just go away. He didn't, of course – he was on a political mission, and his mission happened to be quite profitable. But McDonald's was subjected a multi-million dollar junk science barrage – and a good dose of demonization, too.

Perhaps McDonald's didn't want to draw more attention to Spurlock's film than was already being paid to it; that's the ostrich approach tobacco used for a long time, too. The Center for Consumer Freedom, by contrast, has daily updates and reality checks, debunking the latest junk being served up as science by the CSPI.

Consumer Freedom fights fire with fire, too. They know most people won't read lengthy studies about food additives or trans fats – and, like Spurlock, they know that nothing packs a political wallop like humour and ridicule. They produced and aired a series of ads poking fun at the anti's, including a trial lawyer harassing a girl guide selling cookies. Another ad featured the actor who played the "Soup Nazi" from the TV series *Seinfeld*, the chef who rudely told customers in that show what they could or couldn't order. In the Consumer Freedom ad, the Soup Nazi made restaurant customers stand on a scale, and if they were too heavy, he ordered them to have a salad – or even nothing at all. Other ads are deadly serious, showing the dark side of radical anti-meat groups like People for the Ethical Treatment of Animals, and their support for violence against humans to protect animals.

It's difficult to boil down scientific arguments into slogans short enough for a bumper sticker or even a 30-second ad. But that kind of basic discussion, repeated countless times, is precisely what the anti's are doing. The time to counter false impressions, especially scientific ones, is when they're first being propagated, not once the falsehoods have been swallowed whole by the media and the popular culture.

3. REFRAMING THE BATTLE-LINES

The Center for Consumer Freedom and the SUV Owners of America are effective lobby groups, but they're still lobbyists. Even the most persuasive arguments from lobby groups will inevitably be discounted by the public because of the source.

But the fact is, like the cigarette business, the food and SUV businesses truly are about millions of grassroots shopkeepers, waiters and factory workers. Who meets the definition of the "little guy" better: a Washington lobbyist or a corner store owned by a family that works seven days a week, making money selling chocolate bars and cigarettes?

Groups of anti's always try to define themselves as champions of the downtrodden; it's why they call their opponents big this and big that. But it masks the reality that they are typically lawyers and lobbyists for whom activism is a full-time profession, and who are often funded by highly political foundations – or, as with most anti-smoking organizations, through government tax dollars of one source or another. Can anything more aptly be called "big" than a richly endowed lobby group that forms an NGO to lobby the United Nations to implement regulations on every country in the world?

Fight back groups like Consumer Freedom have their place – there will always be a need for experts, especially to debunk the junk science and to organize the rapid response rebuttals to the Morgan Spurlocks and CSPIs of the world. But the most frequent faces the public should see when the war on fun makes the news are the faces of neighborhood people, severely normal, real life shopkeepers, assembly-line workers and waitresses. Don't put a tobacco spin-doctor on TV to argue against a smoking ban in bars – put on the single mom who pays for her kids' clothes by waitressing for tips. It's not just better optics – it's the face of this war's real victims. The tobacco spin-doctor won't lose his job if the smoking ban goes through; in fact, his job will become even more important. But the waitress really will lose hers. The debate must be reframed. This is not about selfless researchers and public advocates versus big, bad, far-away companies. This is about the convenience store clerk who works 14 hours a day getting laid off because his store can't sell cigarettes anymore and soon candy bars and soft drinks could be restricted to adults, too.

4. TAKE PRO-ACTIVE STEPS WHERE REASONABLE

Already the first battles in the war on food and SUVs have been lost – the public mood is souring on those two industries, and the anti's are building up a head of steam, if not in the courts then certainly in the media. One way for industries to let off some of that steam is to proactively take reasonable, voluntary steps that show goodwill to the public, and take away the anti's righteous indignation.

In the case of cigarettes, the example of ventilating bars comes to mind, as with the Black Dog bar in Toronto. It wasn't an expensive project, but it met the anti-smoking argument head on – and customers fell in love with it. In the end, political opinion was so hardened against smoking that even that sensible solution was rejected without consideration by city's health officers. But it was a great way to voluntarily meet some legitimate market demands, and take away momentum from the anti's.

Examples are becoming more plentiful in the fast-food restaurant industry; McDonald's, for instance, has a variety of salads in their menu, something that didn't exist before *Super Size Me*. They still sell their Big Macs and sundaes, but a good-faith critic would have to concede that McDonald's now has healthy choices on their menu – and it is up to individual customers to exercise their responsibility.

Naturally, that's not what the anti-food nuts want; they want all fatty or sweet foods banned completely – as CSPI motto says, willpower and personal responsibility are not enough. But by providing salads and fruits for dessert, McDonald's gets a public relations win, takes away a reason for politicians to pass invasive laws and, perhaps most importantly, supplies what its customers demand.

The same can be seen in the SUV market, too – while demand continues for extra large SUVs, mini-SUV models are plentiful, including even at GM's Hummer division, the granddaddy of the large SUV-makers. Its H3 model is the smallest yet – nearly one ton lighter than the popular H2, and barely half the weight of the four-ton H1 Alpha model that launched the series.[126] Doubtless the H3 is a response to consumer demand for an easier to park, easier to drive Hummer for cities – and it's a lot cheaper, too. But by bringing in a more modest, fuel-efficient model on its own volition, Hummer has taken some of the rationale away from Hummer-haters – and has met its customers' needs at the same time.

5. SELF-CONFIDENCE

What do the previous four strategies have in common? None of them concede the moral high ground to the anti's. Propaganda from anti-smoking, anti-food and anti-SUV organizations all has the same moral preening to it – a certainty of righteousness and superiority. Arianna Huffington and her Hollywood chums don't have a lot in common with the angry vegetarians at the CSPI, except that they both see themselves as virtuous prophets, living on a higher moral plane than the rest of us. And there's nobody more self-righteous than an anti-smoking crusader.

That kind of baseless self-confidence – or bluster, if you prefer – can be intimidating for people who are less messianic in their self-image. Corporate executives genuinely trying to make food healthier are probably more likely to be self-critical than Hollywood starlets or national politicians looking for a headline. When normal people are attacked for their motives and ethics, they stop and consider the criticisms, especially if they're backed up with "research." Sometimes people who make cigarettes, food and SUVs actually begin to wonder if the anti's aren't as morally superior as they claim they are. But in the game of public perception, a morally strident anti on the attack with incendiary one-liners will beat a thoughtful tobacconist who makes certain logical concessions in the interest of intellectual honesty.

It's not just people acting in good faith who concede the moral high ground to the anti's; sometimes industries know that they're being shaken down by charlatans like Morgan Spurlock, but they just don't know how to, or are plain old afraid to fight back.

The message that sends is destructive to the public debate. The anti's and their supporters are confirmed in their righteousness (after all, the tobacco/food/SUV companies did concede that the anti's motivations/principles were morally superior) and those who are part of the industry are demoralized, or even come to believe that they are evil (if the industry's advocates themselves don't defend the industry, then it must be indefensible).

The war on fun won't be beat back unless those under attack first believe in the nobility of their industries, and the morality of the free market that allows men and women to make choices for themselves – choices that others might disagree with, and even choices that might not be the healthiest choices. It is a risky system, trusting every adult to do what he or she judges to be right for his or herself. But it is far less risky than placing all of our lives and our private, daily decisions about what to eat, smoke and drive under the authority of some all-seeing, all-knowing nanny state.

The battle for freedom of choice in tobacco is not actually about that weed itself, but about our freedom to choose to live our lives in accordance with our own principles, and to have the right to dissent from official views about what is best for us. It is exactly the same battle as the battle for the freedom to eat what we like or drive what we like – and the fact that standing up for tobacco freedom is so politically and fashionably difficult is a sign that our other liberties are in greater jeopardy than we probably realize.

What is at stake is the right to be left alone, and it is a right that both conservatives and liberals ought to share. Liberals ought to remember the root of that word – it is Latin for freedom – and remember their battles for privacy and personal autonomy of the 1960s and 70s. Conservatives ought to remember that giving the state the power to legislate morality is seldom a power that will be limited in its use. And telling a generation of adults that they do not need to take responsibility for their own choices, but rather their tobacconist or restaurateur or auto dealer is to blame for their life's woes, is a most unconservative idea, and one that destroys character.

Freedom to smoke may yet return to North America, as the freedom to drink did after Prohibition. But, for now, it seems far more likely that the forces that conspired to destroy tobacco freedom are planning to continue to expand that battle deeper into our lives, and they'll call upon every tool at their disposal.

The war on fun is blazing away. If you think you're not a target, well, then, you're halfway to losing the battle already.

Endnotes:

[1] Matthew Weiler, personal interview, March 7, 2003.

[2] Table 21, *Smoke-filled Rooms*, W. Kip Viscusi, The University of Chicago Press, 2002, p. 155

[3] *Ibid.*

[4] Contract between Public Works and Government Services Canada and Environics Research Group, as amended December 22, 1998

[5] Environics Research Group, "Focus Group Report to Health Canada – Office for Tobacco Control on Attitudes Towards 'Light' and 'Mild' Cigarettes," January, 1999, p. 4

[6] Ministerial Advisory Committee, "Tobacco Control Strategy", Working Group on Mass Media Social Marketing Commentary Discussion Paper, July, 2001, p. 4

[7] Environics, January 1999, p. 4

[8] Donna M. Owens, "A Conversation with Peter Angelos", *Baltimore Sun*, November 18, 2002

[9] More Dumb Lawsuits, *Washington Post*, April 23, 2001; Page A14

[10] *Mother Jones*, March 5, 2001

[11] "Judge removes himself from asbestos trials", *Prince George Country Journal*, Aug. 2, 2000

[12] "Tip Solves Wendy's Finger Case", CBS News website, May 14, 2005

[13] http://www.horwitzlaw.com/set/ladder.html

[14] "Anti-Industry Propaganda is Constitutionally Suspect," Legal Opinion Letter, Washington Legal Foundation, March 5, 1993

[15] King James I, *The Counterblaste to Tobacco*, London, Robert Barker, Publisher, 1604

[16] *A Law of James about Tobacco*, October 17, 1604

[17] As cited by Robert N. Proctor, *The Nazi War on Cancer*, Princeton University Press, 1999 p. 219

[18] *Ibid.*, pp. 220-221

[19] *Ibid.*, p. 228

[20] *Ibid.*, pp. 234-235

[21] *Ibid.*, p. 132

[22] Pete Sarsfield, CTV, January 2, 2003

[23] CBC *The National*, March 22, 2000

[24] *Ibid.*

[25] Mike Kennedy, CTV, January 7, 2002

[26] Robert Cushman, CTV, August 2, 2001

27 Cathy Backinger, CTV, December 28, 2000

28 Tanya Larsen, CTV, January 16, 2000

29 Colin Gray, CTV, January 16, 2000

30 Richard Stanwick, CTV, January 7, 1999

31 Christine Page, CBC *The National*, December 31, 1998

32 Sidalia Lynne, CBC *The National*, December 31, 1998

33 Eleni Kountourogiannis, CTV, March 24, 1997

34 Rex Murphy, CBC-TV, April 16, 1998

35 "Smoke and Power", Bob Herbert, *The New York Times*, May 26, 2003.

36 http://www.smokefree.ca/eng_home/pschome_about.htm

37 Cynthia Callard, memo to Elizabeth Lindsay, September 20, 1999

38 Cynthia Callard, memo to Janet Davies, May 5, 1999

39 Sandie Rinaldo, CTV, January 19, 2002.

40 Cynthia Callard, letter to Les Hagen, April 12, 1999

41 Garfield Mahood, "Indoor Air," Non-Smokers Rights Association newsletter, June, 1994, p. 9

42 http://tc.bmjjournals.com/misc/echoice3.shtml

[43] David Olive, *Just Rewards;* Key Porter Books, 1987, p. 169

[44] *Ibid.,* p. 173

[45] www.boxofficemojo.com

[46] Ezra Levant, "Who is Jeffrey Wigand", *Calgary Herald,* December 26, 1999, p. A37

[47] http://www.canoe.ca/Health9912/07_smoking2.html Anne Dawson, Sun Media, "The insider scoop", December 5, 1999

[48] Suein L. Hwang and Milo Geyelin, "Getting personal", *Wall Street Journal,* February 1, 1996

[49] CBC Marketplace, October 29, 2002

[50] John Banzhaf, CTV, March 29, 2002

[51] Eric Schlosser, CTV, March 5, 2002

[52] John Schaafsma, CTV, July 24, 2001

[53] Robert Dent, CTV, July 24, 2001

[54] Allan Rock, CTV News, July 24, 2001

[55] Harish Bahrti, CBC TV, May 24, 2001

[56] Bill C-398, *An Act to amend the Food and Drugs Act (food labelling),* 2nd Session, 37th Parliament, 51-52 Elizabeth II,

2002-2003

[57] Extra online, Wednesday, June 20, 2002

[58] http://www.worldnetdaily.com/news/article.asp? ARTI-CLE_ID=30412

[59] http://www.activistcash.com/biography.cfm/bid/2807

[60] http://www.fenton.com/pages/4_news/prweek_jen-nings.htm

[61] http://www.alertnet.org/thenews/newsdesk/N09407143.htm

[62] http://www.fenton.com/pages/3_ourwork/1_clients/clients.htm#Environment

[63] Fenton Fundamentals, December 17, 2002

[64] Letter from Thomas Mason to Kenneth Cleaver, December 2, 2002

[65] http://www.prnewswire.com/cgibin/stories.pl?ACCT=104&STORY=/www/story/08272003/0002007143&EDATE=

[66] *High and Mighty,* p. 417

[67] *Ibid.,* p. 101

[69] *Ibid.,* p. 101

[69] *Ibid.,* p. 101

[70] January 12, 2001 *Federal Register*, fatality rates for 1991-1998

[71] "Putting the crash compatibility issue in perspective," *Status Report*, Vol. 34, No. 9, October 30, 1999

[72] "Death by the Gallon," *USA Today*, 1999

[73] http://www.eia.doe.gov/emeu/aer/pdf/pages/sec5_11.pdf

[74] http://www.dfaitmaeci.gc.ca/middle_east/saudi_arabia_relationsen.asp

[75] http://www.fueleconomy.gov/feg/FEG2005_GasolineVehicles.pdf

[76] http://www.fueleconomy.gov/feg/FEG2000_Part2.pdf

[77] U.S. Environmental Protection Agency, "Light Truck Standards for Hydrocarbon and Nitrogen Oxide Emissions, 1967-2008"

[78] Dan Matheson, CTV, January 13, 2000

[79] Clustering of Fast-Food Restaurants Around Schools: A Novel Application of Spatial Statistics to the Study of Food Environments Austin et al. *Am J Public Health* 2005; 95: 1575-1581.

[80] http://www.cspinet.org/about/funding.html

[81] http://www.activistcash.com/organization_overview.cfm/oid/13

82 *Nutrtion Action Healthletter*, January 2003

83 http://www.hcsc.gc.ca/fnan/foodguidealiment/index_ e.html

84 http://www.mypyramid.gov/

85 Animal Rights 2005 National Conference, arconference.org

86 http://www.cspinet.org/booze/drugwar.htm

87 *Nutrition Action Healthletter*, November 1992

88 http://www.cspinet.org/booze/liquor_branded_press.htm

89 "Take a Kid to a Beer: How the NCAA recruits kids for the beer market", Amy E. Gotwals et al., CSPI, 2005

90 *Washingtonian*, February 1994

91 http://www.cspiscam.com/victims.cfm

92 Joey Green, *The Warning Label Book*, St. Martin's Griffin, 1998

93 Marianne Lavelle, "A Hand in Everything," *U.S. News and World Report*, June 18, 2001

94 http://www.cfsan.fda.gov/~dms/flltr65.html Letter to Bill Lockyer from Lester M. Crawford, Commissioner of Food and Drugs, August 12, 2005

[95] "Aunt Jemima to Correct Labels for "Blueberry" Waffles, August 11, 2005

[96] "Pestering Parents", CSPI, November, 2003

[97] "Purveyors of Junk Food, Kids' TV and Films Presume to Teach Healthy Eating to Children," October 27, 2004 press release, CSPI

[98] Sodium Levels in Processed Foods, August 2005, CSPI

[99] "Systemic review of long term effects of advice to reduce dietary salt in adults", Lee Hooper et al., *British Medical Journal*, 2002; 325:628

[100] "Salt, Blood Pressure and Human Health", Michael Alderman, *Hypertension*, 2000; 36:890

[101] Ezra Levant, *Fight Kyoto*, 2002, JMCK Publishing, p. 85

[102] "The Cooling World," *Newsweek*, April 28,1975

[103] *Fight Kyoto*, p. 224

[104] *Ibid.*, p. 77

[105] *Ibid.*, p. 93

[106] *Ibid.*, p. 73

[107] *Science*, Vol. 294, November 16, 2001

[108] "Fatter kids? Fat chance", Dr. John Luik, *Western Standard*, May 2, 2005

[109] *Ibid.*

[110] "Pop goes the science", John Luik, *Western Standard,* September 5

[111] *Passive Smoke: The EPA's Betrayal of Science and Policy,* Gio B. Gori and John C. Luik, 1999, The Fraser Institute, p. xiii

[112] Flue-cured Tobacco Cooperative Stabilization Corporation et al. v. United States Environmental Protection Agency and Carol Browner, Administrator, Environmental Protection Agency, U.S. District Court, Middle District of North Carolina, Winston-Salem Division, July 17, 1998, Judge William Osteen, at p. 81

[113] *Ibid.,* p. 89

[114] "Environmental tobacco smoke and tobacco related mortality in a prospective study of Californians 1960-98", James E. Enstrom, Geoffrey C. Kabat, *British Medical Journal,* Volume 326, May 17, 2003

[115] "Ventilation blows away smoking issues in restaurants," Venmar corporate newsletter, October 1999

[116] http://blackdogpub.com/welcome.html

[117] March 17, 2000 memo by Ian Potter, http://www.ocat.org/ventilation/solution.html

[118] *Canada Gazette*, "Notice of intent to regulate greenhouse gas emissions by Large Final Emitters", Vol. 139, No. 29, July 16, 2005

[119] Tom Wappel, *Hansard*, February 6, 2004

[120] Robert Merrifield, *Hansard*, February 6, 2004

[121] Tom Wappel, *Hansard*, February 6, 2004

[122] Comments of the International Association of Consumer Food Organizations Round-Table Discussion on the WHO Global Strategy on Diet, Physical Activity and Health, Geneva, Switzerland, March 23, 2005

[123] *Ibid.*, Legal Analysis of WHO's Jurisdiction over Food Regulation p. 10

[124] *Ibid.*, Legal Analysis of WHO's Jurisdiction over Food Regulation p. 12.

[125] http://boxofficemojo.com/genres/chart/?id=documentary.htm

[126] www.hummer.com

YES! Subscribe to Canada's only independent newsmagazine

Read all the exciting news and views everyone is talking about.

BONUS: FREE GIANT-SIZED LIBRANOS POSTER INSIDE

- [ ] 1 Year (24 issues) $80.25—$3.34 per issue
- [ ] 2 Years (48 issues) $154.08—$3.21 per issue
- [ ] 3 Years (72 issues) $211.86—$2.94 per issue
- [ ] 4 Years (96 issues) $256.80—$2.68 per issue
- [ ] 5 Years (120 issues) $288.90—$2.41 per issue

NAME _____

ADDRESS _____

CITY _____ PROVINCE _____ POSTAL CODE _____

E-MAIL _____

IN CANADA CALL 1-866-520-5222. FOR USA AND INTERNATIONAL ORDERS CALL 403-216-2270, ASK FOR OPERATOR 237.

VISIT US ONLINE! www.westernstandard.ca

Please tear out and mail in this coupon to start your subscription to:

WESTERN STANDARD
205-1550 FIFTH STREET SW
CALGARY, ALBERTA   T2R 1K3